商务英语系列课程教材

市场营销英语
English for Marketing

刘亮星　编著

清华大学出版社
北京交通大学出版社
·北京·

内 容 简 介

　　本教材是一本专门用途英语教材,设计理念是以专业知识为载体,学习该领域内的核心及常用语言知识,包括专业词汇、表达、术语、修辞手法、文本写作等。本教材以市场营销的核心知识为纲,包含 14 个单元,主要内容包括营销组合、SWOT 分析、营销战略、营销道德、营销环境、营销法律、营销调查、新产品开发、产品生命周期、品牌建设、市场细分、顾客需求、顾客忠诚、客户关系管理等。本教材选材新颖,素材均选自市场营销领域的专业文章,语言专业地道,编排严谨,练习多样化,涵盖了阅读、口语、写作等各个方面。

　　本教材既适合市场营销、电子商务、工商管理等专业的本科生学习使用,也适合商务英语、国际商务等专业的本科学生选用。

本书封面贴有清华大学出版社防伪标签,无标签者不得销售。
版权所有,侵权必究。侵权举报电话:010-62782989　13501256678　13801310933

图书在版编目（CIP）数据

市场营销英语 / 刘亮星编著. — 北京：北京交通大学出版社 ：清华大学出版社,2022.12
ISBN 978-7-5121-4866-6

Ⅰ. ① 市… Ⅱ. ① 刘… Ⅲ. ① 市场营销–英语–高等学校–教材 Ⅳ. ① F713.3

中国版本图书馆 CIP 数据核字（2022）第 251674 号

市场营销英语
SHICHANG YINGXIAO YINGYU

责任编辑：张利军

出版发行：	清 华 大 学 出 版 社	邮编：100084	电话：010-62776969	http://www.tup.com.cn
	北京交通大学出版社	邮编：100044	电话：010-51686414	http://www.bjtup.com.cn

印　刷　者：北京鑫海金澳胶印有限公司
经　　　销：全国新华书店
开　　　本：185 mm×260 mm　　印张：15.75　　字数：395 千字
版 印 次：2022 年 12 月第 1 版　　2022 年 12 月第 1 次印刷
定　　　价：49.00 元

本书如有质量问题,请向北京交通大学出版社质监组反映。对您的意见和批评,我们表示欢迎和感谢。
投诉电话：010-51686043,51686008；传真：010-62225406；E-mail：press@bjtu.edu.cn

前言

本教材是国家级一流本科课程（线上类）"市场营销英语"的配套教材。

在全球化背景下，为了实现产业转型升级、加快国内企业走出去的步伐、扩大及加深国内企业在国际经济活动中的参与度，国家提出"一带一路"倡议（the Belt and Road Initiative）。为实现这一宏伟愿景，国家急需大量既掌握专业理论知识和技能，又能熟练使用专业外语与外国专业人士进行沟通的复合型人才。这本教材就是在这样的背景下应运而生的。

这是一本适合市场营销电子商务、工商管理等专业本科学生或商务英语学习者使用的专门用途英语（English for Specific Purposes）教材。编者挑选市场营销专业入门必学的核心内容，采用编者自己撰写或改编的原版文章，按照主题及其关联逻辑进行编排，并对关键专业术语及词汇进行匹配度较高的解释及练习，以帮助学习者更高效地学习其中的内容。

为了体现"英语语言＋专业知识"的特点，本教材精心设计了专门的语言练习和专业知识练习。因此，本教材的特点是：在简单明了、由浅入深地介绍市场营销知识及行业案例的同时，还可以帮助读者增加营销领域内的英语词汇量，提高读者的英语阅读水平和专业口头沟通能力。

本教材体例清晰，结构明了，易于操作。在编写本教材时，编者为了适应中国学生的学习特点和习惯，做出了以下安排：

第一，每个单元设有相应的学习目标（Learning Objectives），让学习者明白自己需要学到什么。

第二，每个单元设有课前思考题、讨论题（Pre-class Questions），鼓励学习者进行热身讨论。

第三，每个单元都包含三篇文章：第一篇是导入文章（Text A: Lead-in），短小精悍，配有词汇表（Vocabulary and Useful Expressions）及相关的语言练习（Language Exercise）和专业知识练习（Knowledge Exercise），全部都以英文呈现，该部分内容旨在引导学生进入该主题的学习；第二篇是精读文章（Text B: Intensive Reading），内容涉及该单元专业话题的讨论，配有词汇表、各种不同形式的语言练习和专业知识练习，

I

以及有详细指引的口语训练任务，内容丰富，适合老师带领学生仔细学习；第三篇是拓展阅读（Text C: Extensive Reading），基本以迷你案例（Mini Case）为主，要求学习者在阅读案例的基础上，自行搜索、阅读相关行业案例，并参照案例格式完成写作任务。

第四，在给学生布置的写作任务中，编者根据章节主题及内容的不同灵活设置相应的任务，如撰写营销组合分析报告、撰写市场细分分析报告、撰写某公司的SWOT分析报告等，以帮助学生接触不同类别的内容，开阔眼界。

本教材既可用于市场营销专业英语或者双语课程的教学，也可以作为从事营销相关工作的英语爱好者的阅读学习材料。

此外，本教材还以二维码的形式向读者提供相关的教学资源，读者可先扫描书后的防盗码获得资源读取权限，然后再扫描书中每单元 Text A、Text B、Text C 开始处的二维码来获取相应的教学资源。

本教材可以结合慕课课程"市场营销英语"进行线上线下混合式教学，也可以独立用于线下课堂教学。

对于如何使用本教材，编者建议如下。

如果进行线上线下混合式教学，教师可要求学生先完成线上部分的内容，再安排2个线下课时，检测学生的在线学习成果，并根据本教材 Text A 和 Text B 的内容，加深学生对该单元语言知识和专业知识的理解和掌握，最后安排2个课时，专门组织口语及写作活动。

如果进行纯线下教学，教师可以完全根据教材内容，逐步带领学生由浅入深地进行学习。教师可以根据面授学生的实际能力和水平来选取内容：如果学生水平较高，则可以在前2个课时内 Text A 和 Text B 都讲；如果学生水平较为一般，则可以选择只讲 Text A 及其配套练习，后2个课时用来完成 Text C 的阅读，组织学生分组讨论、分析案例及进行写作练习。

需要特别说明的是，教师在使用此书时，应根据不同的教学对象和不同的课程性质（全英课或双语课）灵活调配各个教学环节所占的比重，以期达到最佳的教学效果。

在这里特别感谢广东外语外贸大学英语教育学院原院长董金伟教授、广东外语外贸大学教务部部长陈金诗教授，正是在他们的关注、关心、督促、鼓励和指导下，才有了这本教材的成型和出版；感谢郑州大学体育学院杨慧老师详细校对了本教材的初稿，提出了不少修改意见；感谢王慕雪女士为本教材精心绘制了相关插图；感谢我的家人对我一贯的支持和鼓励！

由于编者的学识及编写时间有限，教材中仍可能存在错漏之处，还请读者谅解并希望能不吝指出。非常感谢！

编者

2022年12月

目 录

Unit 1	The Marketing Mix	1
Unit 2	SWOT Analysis	17
Unit 3	Marketing Strategy	33
Unit 4	Marketing Ethics	49
Unit 5	Marketing Environment	63
Unit 6	Legal Aspects of Marketing	79
Unit 7	Marketing Research	93
Unit 8	New Product Development	111
Unit 9	Product Life Cycle	125
Unit 10	Branding	141
Unit 11	Market Segmentation	157
Unit 12	Customer Needs	173
Unit 13	Customer Loyalty	189
Unit 14	Customer Relationship Management	207
Appendix A	Glossary	225

Unit 1

The Marketing Mix

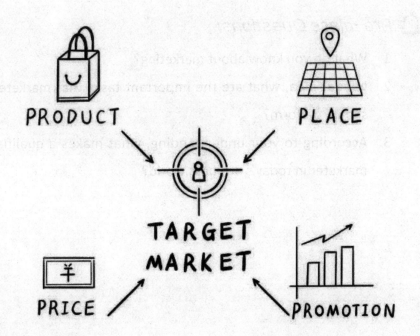

🔔 Quote of the Unit:

"The aim of marketing is to know and understand the customer so well that the product or service fits him and sells itself."

—Peter Drucker, founder of Drucker Institute

🔔 Learning Objectives:

1. Understand some basic concepts of marketing and marketing mix.
2. Understand the key characteristics of a modern marketer.
3. Apply both the language and knowledge learned in this unit to analyzing marketing related cases.

🔔 Pre-class Questions:

1. What do you know about marketing?
2. In your idea, what are the important tasks that marketers should perform?
3. According to your understanding, what makes a qualified marketer in today's business world?

Text A: Lead-in

About Marketing Mix

Learning Resources

Marketing mix is normally regarded as a fundamental model in marketing. The word "mix" is **synonymous** with "combination", therefore, marketing mix can be defined as the combination of marketing tools that a firm uses to pursue its marketing objectives.

The term was originally **coined** by Jerome McCarthy, a **pivotal** figure in the development of marketing thinking. Since its coinage, it quickly became one of the most enduring and widely accepted concepts in marketing.

To be specific, the marketing mix refers to four broad levels of marketing decision, namely product, price, place and promotion.

First, product. A product refers to an item that satisfies consumers' needs or wants. In modern sense the boundary between a **tangible** product and an **intangible** service is already blurred. These days people often use the word "product" to refer to their services. A successful product should be one that can satisfy a customer's specific need to solve a real problem. If a product is very good in terms of quality but does not really help solve an **existent** problem for people, it will be less likely to be successful. Besides, when people make product decisions they should also consider the following elements, such as product design, features, quality, branding, and product life cycle issues.

Second, price. Price refers to the amount of money a customer pays for a product. It may also refer to the sacrifice consumers are willing to make in order to obtain a product. It is regarded as the only **variable** that has implications for revenue.

Fixing a price for a product is not an easy task, since decision makers need to take many issues into consideration. For example, sales volume objectives, revenue objectives and profit objectives, etc. In order to make their products more competitive in the marketplace, different companies adopt different pricing strategies, such as premium pricing, penetration pricing, psychological pricing, etc. In practice, many sellers may provide discounts or favorable payment terms to attract customers.

Third, place. Originally place refers to location, logistics, warehousing and distribution. In a broader sense, place also refers to providing customers access to products. Hence, companies should consider improving **accessibility** of their products. The key element of place is convenience, which means a business should consider providing convenience for consumers to reach the product. This is also a very important decision in that if the product is not widely and appropriately distributed then it would lose the favor of consumers, since no one would like to travel a long way to buy something. Therefore, market coverage is a very important issue to consider. Strategies such as intensive distribution, selective distribution, exclusive distribution, franchising are often applied to improving accessibility of products. In the era of Internet, catalogues, credit cards and phones, people neither need to go anywhere to satisfy a want or a need, nor are limited to only a few shopping places. Today, marketers should know how the target market prefers to buy, how to be there and be **ubiquitous**, in order to guarantee convenience to buy.

At last, promotion. It is a marketing communication process that helps publicize a product to the public. It helps grab the attention of the customers and influence or persuade them to buy the product. Marketers use tactics to promote their products and reach out to the target audience. The promotion might include direct marketing, advertising, personal branding, sales promotion, and any form of communication between the organization and the consumers.

While promotion is regarded as "**manipulative**", which means it is initiated by the seller, communication is seen as "cooperative" exchange of information and opinions from the buyers, with the aim to create a dialogue with the potential customers based on their needs and lifestyles. Businesses currently prefer to use socializing Apps to create and distribute messages to target audience, hoping to create a buzz among them.   (642 words)

Vocabulary and Useful Expressions

synonymous /sɪˈnɒnɪməs/	a.	having the same, or nearly the same, meaning 同义的
coin /kɔɪn/	v.	to invent a new word or phrase that other people then begin to use 创造（新词语）
pivotal /ˈpɪvətl/	a.	of great importance because other things depend on it 关键性的，核心的
tangible /ˈtændʒəbl/	a.	that can be clearly seen to exist 有形的，实际的，真实的
intangible /ɪnˈtændʒəbl/	a.	that does not exist as a physical thing but is still valuable to a company 无形的（指没有实体存在的资本性资产）
existent /ɪɡˈzɪstənt/	a.	existing; real 存在的，实有的

Unit 1　The Marketing Mix

variable /ˈvɛərɪəbl/	n.	a situation, number or quantity that can vary or be varied　可变情况，变量，可变因素
accessibility /əkˌsesəˈbɪlətɪ/	n.	the quality of being at hand when needed　易接近，可达性
ubiquitous /juːˈbɪkwɪtəs/	a.	seeming to be everywhere or in several places at the same time; very common　似乎无所不在的，十分普遍的
manipulative /məˈnɪpjʊlətɪv/	a.	if you describe someone as manipulative, you disapprove of them because they skillfully force or persuade people to act in the way that they want　善于操纵的，会控制的，会摆布人的

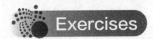

Exercises

Exercise 1. Language: Fill in the blanks with words or expressions from the above article.

1. Promotion is regarded as _____ since it is initiated by marketers. Consumers commonly see it as a trick to lure them into buying products through manipulation.
2. New product development is a process that aims at developing a new product to solve an _____ problem.
3. Price is an important _____ that may influence revenue and profitability.
4. Advertisement is _____ across the globe. It can be seen almost everywhere.
5. Marketers should try every means to improve product _____ so that consumers can buy it without much effort.
6. A physical product is normally seen as _____.
7. Service is traditionally thought as _____.
8. As an old saying goes, wealth is not necessarily _____ with happiness.
9. The marketing mix, which consists of product, price, place and promotion, plays a _____ role in marketing.
10. Researchers try to _____ a term to describe communities of homeless people living in cardboard boxes.

Exercise 2. Knowledge: True or false statements. If the following statements are true, write T; if false, write F.

1. The term marketing mix was originally coined to reflect market situations.　　(　　)

5

2. Marketing mix is the combination of marketing tools to help marketers pursue marketing objectives. ( )
3. The marketing mix is one of the most popular and accepted concepts in marketing. ( )
4. A product is regarded as a solution to a consumer's existent problem. ( )
5. Promotion can be either manipulative or communicative. ( )
6. Pricing decisions can directly affect one company's revenue and profitability. ( )
7. Improving a product's accessibility to consumers is one of the major jobs of marketers. ( )
8. A product is absolutely tangible according to its definition. ( )
9. As a trend, marketers tend to use socializing platforms to promote their products nowadays. ( )
10. In practice many sellers provide discounts or favorable payment terms to attract customers. ( )

Text B: Intensive Reading

Learning Resources

Marketers and Their Roles and Characteristics

Marketing consists of the strategies and tactics used to help marketers identify, create and maintain satisfying, **sustained** and mutually beneficial relationships with customers.

What Marketers Do

In order to reach the goal of creating and maintaining a satisfying, sustained and mutually beneficial relationship that adds value to both customers and the organization, marketers use a diverse **toolkit** that facilitates decision making in the following aspects.

Product — a product can be seen as an item that helps solve a consumer's problem. It can either be a tangible good or an intangible service. Tangible products are those that have an independent physical existence. Typical examples of **mass-produced**, tangible objects are cars and the **disposable** razors. A less obvious but ubiquitous mass-produced service is a computer operating system.

Price — the amount a customer pays for the product. Price is particularly important as it determines the company's profit, and affects its survival and further development. Adjusting the price has a profound impact on the marketing strategy and, in view of the price **elasticity** of the product, price change will affect the demand and sales as well.

Place — place refers to providing the product at a place which is convenient for consumers to access. Various strategies such as intensive distribution, selective distribution, exclusive distribution and **franchising** can be used by marketers to **complement** the other aspects of the marketing mix.

Promotion — all of the methods of communication that a marketer may use to provide information about the product to the public, especially the target audience. Promotion **comprises** elements such as: advertising, public relations, sales organization and sales promotion.

Target Markets — markets consist of customers identified as possessing needs that the marketer believes can be addressed by marketing efforts.

Each option within the marketer's toolkit is tightly **integrated** with all other options so that a decision in one area could impact decisions in other areas. For instance, a change in the price of a product (e.g., lowering the price) could impact distribution (e.g., requires increased product shipments to retail stores).

Additionally, options within the toolkit are affected by factors beyond the control of marketers. These include economic conditions, political/legal issues, technological developments, social/cultural changes, etc. These external factors must be monitored carefully and dealt with since these can either generate opportunities or cause considerable harm to the organization. Ignorance of outside elements will be very costly especially if competitors are the first to take advantage of the opportunities. Therefore, it would be particularly wise for marketers to pay close attention to the changing environment outside the organization.

Characteristics of Modern Marketers

Marketing is a critical business function that operates in an environment which is highly **scrutinized** and constantly changing. Today's marketers should undertake various tasks so that they can build customer relationships, and the knowledge and skill sets needed to successfully perform these tasks are also varied.

Then What Does It Take to Be a Successful Marketer?

Obviously, at the center of a successful marketing career is an understanding of the important concepts of marketing. But basic marketing knowledge is just the beginning, modern marketers must possess much more than that:

Basic Business Skills

Marketers are first and **foremost** business people who must perform necessary tasks required of all successful business people. These basic skills include problem analysis and decision-making, oral and written communication, basic quantitative skills, team spirit and interpersonal skills.

Understanding Marketing's Impact

Marketers must take a wholistic view of the business and know how their decisions will impact other areas of the company and business partners. They must realize that marketing decisions are not made in isolation and that decisions made by the marketing team might possibly lead to problems for others. For example, deciding to run a special sale that significantly lowers the price of a product could lead to supply problems if the production is not informed well in advance of the sale.

Technology Savvy

Today's marketers must have a strong understanding of technology on two fronts. First, marketers must be skilled in using technology as part of their daily activities. Not only must they understand how basic computer software is used to build spreadsheets or create slide presentations, but in a world where information **overload** is a problem. Marketers must investigate additional technologies that can improve their effectiveness and efficiency, such as multifunctional smartphones, web-based **productivity** applications. Second, marketers must understand emerging technology and applications in order to spot potential business opportunities as well as potential threats. For instance, the rapid growth of social media requires marketers to firmly understand how these fit within an overall marketing strategy.

Global Perspective

Thanks to the Internet, it is now theoretically possible for every company to do business on a global scale. Yet, just having a website that is accessible to hundreds of millions of people worldwide does not guarantee success. Marketers selling internationally must understand the nuances of international trade and cultural differences that exist between markets.

Information Seeker

The field of marketing is dynamic. Changes occur constantly and rapidly. Marketers must maintain close contact with these changes through a steady intake of information. Information can be obtained through formal marketing research methods that includes the use of a variety of information gathering techniques. However, marketers also must be in tune with day-to-day developments by paying close attention to news that occurs in their industry, in the markets they serve, and among their potential customers. (900 words)

Vocabulary and Useful Expressions

sustained	/səsˈteɪnd/	a.	maintained at length without interruption or weakening 可持续的，持久的
toolkit	/ˈtuːlkɪt/	n.	a set of tools in a box or bag （装在箱子或包里的）一套工具，工具箱，工具包
mass-produced	/ˌmæs prəˈdjuːst/	a.	if something is mass-produced, it is made in large quantities, usually by machine 大批量生产的
disposable	/dɪˈspəʊzəbl/	a.	made to be thrown away after use 用后即丢弃的，一次性的
elasticity	/ˌiːlæˈstɪsəti/	n.	in economics, the elasticity of something, especially the demand for a product, is the degree to which it changes in response to changes in circumstances （尤指产品需求的）弹性，灵活性，伸缩性
franchising	/ˈfræntʃaɪzɪŋ/	n.	a form of marketing and distribution in which the owner of a business system (the franchisor) grants to an individual or group of individuals (the franchisee) the right to run a business selling a product or providing a service using the franchisor's business system 特许经营
complement	/ˈkɒmplɪment/	v.	to add to sth. in a way that improves it or makes it more attractive 补充，补足，使完美，使更具吸引力
comprise	/kəmˈpraɪz/	v.	if you say that something comprises or is comprised of a number of things or people, you mean it has them as its parts or members 包括，由……组成
integrate	/ˈɪntɪgreɪt/	v.	to combine two or more things so that they work together; to combine with sth. else in this way （使）合并，成为一体
scrutinize	/ˈskruːtənaɪz/	v.	to look at or examine sb./sth. carefully 仔细查看，认真检查，细致审查

foremost /ˈfɔːməʊst/	*a.*	the most important or famous; in a position at the front 最重要的，最著名的，最前的
savvy /ˈsævɪ/	*n.*	(informal) practical knowledge or understanding of sth. 实际知识，见识，了解
overload /ˌəʊvəˈləʊd/	*n.*	too much of sth. 过多，过量，超负荷
productivity /ˌprɒdʌkˈtɪvətɪ/	*n.*	the rate at which a worker, a company or a country produces goods, and the amount produced, compared with how much time, work and money is needed to produce them 生产率，生产效率，生产力
perspective /pəˈspektɪv/	*n.*	a particular attitude towards sth.; a way of thinking about sth. (~ on sth.) 态度，观点，思考方法

Exercise 1. Language: Correct the language mistakes you identify in the following sentences.

1. Typical examples of mass-produced, intangible objects include cars and the disposable razors.

2. Various strategies such as intensive distribution, exclusive distribution and franchising can be used by marketers to compliment the other aspects of the marketing mix.

3. Marketers are firstmost business people who must perform necessary tasks required of all successful business people.

4. Marketers use a diverse toolkit that facilitations decision making in various aspects.

5. Each option within the marketer's toolkit is tightly integrate with all other options so that a decision in one area could impact decisions in other areas.

Unit 1 The Marketing Mix

6. Modern consumers have to face the problem of information overloading, which may cause difficulty of selection for them.
_____
_____

7. Marketing is a critical business function that operates in an environment which is highly scrutinizing and constantly static.
_____
_____

8. Merely constructing a website that is accessibility to hundreds of millions of people worldwide does not guarantee success.
_____
_____

9. In view of the price elastic of the product, price change will affect the demand and sales as well.
_____
_____

10. Computers and smartphones can be regarded as productive tools for modern marketers.
_____
_____

Exercise 2. Knowledge: Answer the following questions briefly according to the above article.

1. Can you define marketing in your own words?
_____

2. How can marketers develop satisfying relationships with customers that benefit both the customers and the organization?
_____
_____

3. When it comes to making product decisions, what factors should marketers consider?
_____
_____

4. When it comes to setting a price for the product, what factors should marketers consider?
_____
_____

5. When it comes to promotion, what methods can be used to promote one organization's products or services?

11

6. When it comes to place (distribution), how can the marketers distribute their products so as to make them more accessible to customers?

7. Why is it necessary for marketers to pay close attention to the changing environment outside the organization?

8. In terms of developing a global perspective, what does a marketer need to pay attention to?

9. In order to develop technology savvy, what should a marketer do?

10. As an information seeker, what types of information must a marketer seek for or collect?

Oral practice: Work in pairs. One part of the article above discusses the characteristics of modern marketers. After reading it carefully, firstly retell the major characteristics to your partner and you may complement them with your own ideas; secondly, rank the characteristics according to their importance and justify this ranking.

Text C: Extensive Reading

Learning Resources

Fast-food Chains in Asia Cater Menus to Customers

By Kathy Chu

HONG KONG SAR — Two floors below ground, in his stainless-steel laboratory, McDonald's food scientist Leslie Bailey creates tempting Asian dishes such as taro pie, mala chicken and wasabi filet of fish.

But his duties in the company's so-called Forbidden Kitchen also involve testing the quality of existing products: hamburgers, fries and condiments. It's a job that requires precision, nuanced taste buds and a healthy appreciation for protein.

"People come to McDonald's expecting a certain taste," says Bailey, explaining why the U.S. fast-food giant obsesses about such details as how much to salt its fries and how much ketchup to apply to its beef patties.

In recent years, fast-growing Asia has become a corporate playground for a host of American industries, especially as business has slowed in the U.S. fast-food companies are no exception. In 2009, fast food — from burgers to tacos to ice cream — generated $139.8 billion in retail sales in Asia Pacific, rising nearly 32% from two years before, says Euromonitor International. By comparison, the larger American fast-food industry grew at a snail's pace, with total sales up 1% to $181.2 billion in that time.

One rule for success in this region? Adhering closely to time-tested recipes while offering the right mix of new products to appeal to Asian palates.

It's a simple, but not easy, formula. Finding this balance "is the biggest problem, challenge and headache for any company," says Martin Roll, a Singapore brand strategist who wrote *Asian Brand Strategy*. "There's no fact sheet on how to do it."

A Marriage of East and West

U.S. companies have been tailoring products to local tastes — and grappling with the challenges inherent in doing so — for decades. What's changed is that in recent years, companies have begun to realize they need to be more sophisticated about their offerings in Asian markets.

In the past, most of what Western companies sold in Asia were the same products offered in the U.S., with "very superficial... cosmetic changes," says David Tse, an international marketing professor at the University of Hong Kong. But as China's economic might has grown, so has American companies' willingness to fundamentally revamp their menus in Asia. "China has become too big to ignore," says Tse.

Yum's KFC, for example, offers a significant number of menu items geared specifically to Asian tastes. In China, the fast-food chain's 3,000 stores serve items such as congee, or rice soup, and the "dragon twister", a tortilla wrap containing crispy chicken strips, cucumber, scallions and Beijing roast duck sauce. Meanwhile, Pizza Hut, also part of Yum, serves up entrées in Asia such as a lemon-flavored salmon pastry roll and a "seafood catch" pizza, topped with crab sticks, green pepper and pineapple.

Locals appear to be embracing the innovations: Since 2005, Yum has added more than 1,800 restaurants and tripled its profits in China and Thailand. The chain is also expanding in established Asian markets such as Hong Kong of China, and up-and-coming ones such as Vietnam.

Starbucks now serves black sesame green tea and Frappuccinos with coffee jelly pieces in Asia. For years after Starbucks entered the Asia-Pacific market it offered products similar to its U.S. stores. But Starbucks has increasingly tailored its menu to Asian tastes amid fierce competition from local brands.

Meanwhile, General Mills' Häagen-Dazs premium ice cream brand, which has 140 shops in the greater China region, not only offers fruity flavors (which tend to appeal to consumers here) but sells special products for Asian holidays.

They Want to Be Part of It

Häagen-Dazs is marketing a twist on traditional dough-and-egg cakes given to family and friends during the mid-autumn moon festival. Häagen-Dazs' full moon-shaped concoction has ice cream and also may have wafers, caramel or a chocolate coating.

"The ice cream moon cake has become major business," says Gary Chu, president of the greater China region for General Mills. Häagen-Dazs expects to sell 1.5 million boxes of moon cakes in the region this year, up 20% from 2009. Yet, it still has work to do in winning customers. "I like the traditional moon cakes," says Horace Cheng, 20, as he enjoyed a rum raisin ice cream cone at a Häagen-Dazs shop in Hong Kong. Häagen-Dazs' version "is just ice cream".

General Mills also has adapted snacks such as its Bugles chips to local tastes. In Asia, the company makes the snacks out of rice and potato, in addition to corn, the ingredient used in the U.S. It also offers flavors such as ketchup and seaweed. "You really have to understand the local customer," Chu says.

While U.S. companies have become smarter about catering to Asian markets, they've been able to do so only through a process of trial and error.

A few years ago, McDonald's offered a rice burger — a meat patty sandwiched by sticky rice molded into a bun — in Singapore, the Philippines and Hong Kong SAR of China. Customers initially responded favorably to the product but eventually lost interest because rice is not something they associate with McDonald's, says Tim Fenton, the chain's president for the Asia, Pacific, Middle East and Africa region. "Customers come to us because they want us to be McDonald's, and when we try to become something we're not, they don't like it." Yet, what Asian customers welcome, Fenton adds, is when the company takes a familiar product and "puts a local twist on it".

Roll, the brand consultant, warns that Western brands can go overboard in their attempts to adapt to Asian tastes. "My experience is that if people see you as too local, why would they buy your brand versus the local brand? You risk losing your identity and what you stand for in the first place."

But Tse disagrees, saying a concept will fail if it's ill conceived, not because the product is too responsive to local tastes. "I've never seen any product over-adapt and destroy the brand," he says.   (990 words)

(**Source:** http://usatoday30.usatoday.com/money/world/2010-09-07-asiatastes07_ST_N.htm.)

Knowledge: Answer the following questions briefly according to the above article.

1. Can you list the marketing mix (or 4Ps) of any one of the aforementioned companies?

2. How do these companies adapt to the marketplace? How do their actions embody the marketing concepts that you learned previously?

3. Do you think these tactical changes would help these companies win greater popularity among Asian customers? You can illustrate your answer to this question by using your own experience.

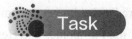

Oral practice: Work in pairs. Suppose you (Student A) are an international business consultant. An executive (Student B) of an international fast food chain wants to know more about how to enter the Chinese market, and how to organize the marketing mix of the company.

Direction:
Student B should introduce the general situation of the fast food chain, including its brief history, its main products, and its main target markets.

Student A should try to introduce the characteristics of the Chinese market, and preferences of Chinese customers. At the same time, Student A should provide specific suggestions on how to make changes to Student B's marketing mix.

At last, the two students should summarize the content of the discussion and report it to the teacher orally.

Writing: Read more cases about how international firms adapt their marketing mix to cater to Chinese customers, and write a brief report about their actions, how they change the marketing mix (especially the specific 4Ps in the marketing mix), and the result of these changes.

Word limit: 250 words.

Unit 2

SWOT Analysis

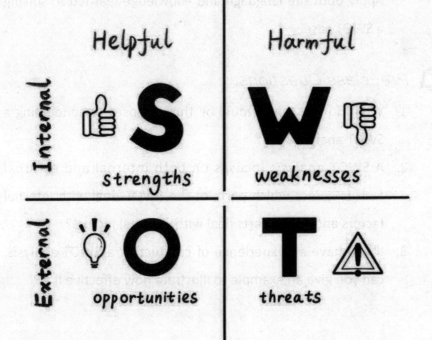

Quote of the Unit:

"If you know the enemy and know yourself, you need not fear the result of a hundred battles. If you know yourself but not the enemy, for every victory gained you will also suffer a defeat. If you know neither the enemy nor yourself, you will succumb in every battle."

—Sun Tzu, *The Art of War*

Learning Objectives:

1. Understand the essential concepts and categorization of SWOT items.
2. Understand the language used in describing a SWOT analysis.
3. Apply both the language and knowledge learned to solving a SWOT case.

Pre-class Questions:

1. What do you think would be the purposes of conducting a SWOT analysis?
2. A SWOT analysis focuses on both internal and external factors, guess which parts of the SWOT deal with internal factors and which parts deal with external factors?
3. If you have an experience of conducting a SWOT analysis, can you give an example to illustrate how effective it is?

Text A: Lead-in

Learning Resources

Synergy E-Car®, a start-up electric car manufacturer based in China, is holding a public relations event. Dr. Alex Chen, the company's CEO, makes a presentation in front of a group of **stakeholders** to illustrate the company's its business situation. The following is part of his presentation.

Good morning, ladies and gentlemen! Welcome to Synergy E-Car!

Last year, our company has witnessed rapid development of the market for electric car in China. It is a **blessing** for us, since we have achieved a major increase in both sales volume and net profits. However, it also poses a challenge to us, considering this segment is already attractive enough to lure more new **entrants** to rush in, bringing more competition for all players present.

Then what about us? How **poised** are we to meet the challenges?

First of all, let me talk about our strengths. Our main strength comes from our major product. We offer luxury high-performance electric cars. It means that our customers can drive an environmentally-friendly car without sacrificing performance or **chic** looks. Our cars are absolutely beautifully designed and **exhilarating** to drive, at the same time the driver saves money on petrol. Our customers are happy because it costs them about a tenth of the money to run an electric sports car compared with a petrol one.

Our technological **know-how** is another strength. So, for example, the batteries that we've designed allow our cars to travel over 400 kilometers between two charges: that's more than any other electric car available on the market.

However, some people take it as a potential weakness. For customers who already drive an electric car, 400 kilometers is already good, but what if compared with a regular sports car, say, a Ferrari, a Porsche that can travel a lot further than 400 kilometers before they need to stop at a petrol station?

I have to further admit, high price is another of our weaknesses, and that's mainly because our manufacturing and high-tech material costs are so high. Our cheapest model currently is sold at RMB 240,00 yuan. And there are some external issues affecting that market negatively, too.

19

As for threats, it may be that once electric car technology becomes more mainstream and cheaper, then barriers to entry will be lower. There will be more competitors, as I have mentioned earlier at the very beginning. And there's the global economic downturn. It's affecting how much people are willing to spend, especially when it comes to luxury goods such as sports cars. But that could present some opportunities as well: traditional big car manufacturers like Volkswagen, Ford, GM, etc. will probably avoid a high-risk market like ours and concentrate on the mass market instead; that spells less competition for us.

Additionally, the government's electric cars **incentive scheme** is designed to encourage mass-market electric cars, which won't spell more competition for the company. Though it may help reduce the barriers to entry, in the meanwhile, the company will still be able to benefit from the increase of investment in electric car **infrastructure** construction such as more charging points and battery-changing stations, as well as rising public awareness of electric cars. We might also be able to get some of that RMB100 million yuan in investment money from the government.

At the same time, yuan is currently weak against other major currencies, and the trend will likely continue into the following years, which means it will be cheaper for customers in Europe and the US to buy cars imported from China. So that's an opportunity if we move into European and American markets. (597 words)

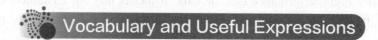

Vocabulary and Useful Expressions

stakeholder /ˈsteɪkhəʊldə(r)/	n.	a person or company that is involved in a particular organization, project, system, etc., especially because they have invested money in it （某组织、工程、体系等的）参与人，参与方，有权益关系者，利益相关者
blessing /ˈblesɪŋ/	n.	something that is good or helpful 好事，有益之事
entrant /ˈentrənt/	n.	a person or an animal that enters a race or a competition; a person that enters an exam 参赛者（或动物），考生
poised /pɔɪzd/	a.	completely ready for sth. or to do sth. 有充分准备，准备好，蓄势待发
chic /ʃiːk/	a.	very fashionable and elegant 时髦的，优雅的，雅致的

exhilarating /ɪgˈzɪləreɪtɪŋ/	a.	very exciting and enjoyable 使人兴奋的，令人激动的	
know-how /ˈnəʊ haʊ/	n.	knowledge of the methods or techniques of doing something, especially something technical or practical 专门知识，技能，实际经验	
incentive /ɪnˈsentɪv/	n.	something that encourages you to do sth. (~ for/to sb./sth.; ~ to do sth.) 激励，刺激，鼓励	
scheme /skiːm/	n.	(British English) a plan or system for doing or organizing sth. 计划，方案，体系，体制	
infrastructure /ˈɪnfrəstrʌktʃə(r)/	n.	the basic systems and services that are necessary for a country or an organization to run smoothly, for example buildings, transport and water and power supplies （国家或机构的）基础设施，基础建设	

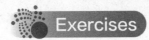

Exercise 1. Knowledge: Sort out the SWOT factors according to Dr. Chen's presentation, and put them into the following matrix respectively.

S:	W:
① _____	① _____
② _____	② _____
③ _____	③ _____
O:	T:
① _____	① _____
② _____	② _____
③ _____	③ _____

Exercise 2. Language: Choose the right words to fill in the blanks.

infrastructure	incentive	stakeholder	blessing
charging	exhilarating	scheme	poised

1. The company offers a bonus as an _____ to greater speed and efficiency in production.
2. We need to invest in _____ for electric vehicles since the market is increasing fast but not fast enough to prevent further climate changes.
3. Employees are internal _____ because they are directly affected by the decisions of management.
4. Apple's newly revealed iOS 16 offers mixed _____ for marketers who need to interact with consumers on mobile.
5. The Chinese government has been dedicated to formulating standards to make electric vehicle _____ stations more accessible to drivers.
6. My first test drive of an electric vehicle was really an _____ experience.
7. A loyalty _____ is uniquely designed for encouraging consumers to have a connection to a particular brand and encourage repeat business.
8. After a longtime hardship and difficulty, the economy is now _____ for recovery.

Text B: Intensive Reading

Learning Resources

SWOT Analysis: What It Is and When to Use It

A SWOT analysis is a strategic planning technique that helps outline an organization's strengths, weaknesses, opportunities, and threats. The primary objective of a SWOT analysis is to help organizations develop a full awareness of all the factors involved in making a business decision. Since its creation, SWOT has become one of the most useful tools for business owners to start and develop their companies.

When Should You Perform a SWOT Analysis?

SWOT analysis can be employed before committing to any sort of company action, whether you are exploring new **initiatives**, **revamping** internal policies or considering an alteration of a current plan midway through execution. Sometimes it's wise to perform a general SWOT analysis just to check on the current **landscape** of the business so you can improve business operations **contingent** upon the results.

The analysis can show you the key areas where your organization is performing optimally, as well as which operations need adjustment. By taking the time to conduct a formal SWOT analysis, you can see the whole picture of your business. From there, one can discover ways to improve the company's weaknesses, **circumvent** threats and **leverage** its strengths to seize business opportunities.

A SWOT analysis is most effective when it collects a full **spectrum** of perspectives by assessing the business in a brutally honest way. Gathering key stakeholders with various perspectives will help you see more than you would have seen alone: marketing leaders might be able to give you a more specific sense of the opportunities and threats related to your marketing efforts; your people team is closest to all personnel changes and feedback, so they'll have the clearest sense of an organization's strengths and what is driving or challenging employee retention; sales leaders can help translate opportunities into a cohesive business strategy.

Characteristics of a SWOT Analysis

A SWOT analysis allows companies to identify the major forces influencing company strategies, initiatives or actions. Knowing these positive and negative elements can help companies more effectively communicate what parts of a plan need to be identified and addressed.

When it comes to drafting a SWOT analysis, participants typically create a table split into four columns to list each impacting element side by side for comparison. Strengths and weaknesses won't typically match opportunities and threats verbatim, although they should correlate. Pairing external threats with internal weaknesses can highlight the most serious issues a company faces.

Internal Factors

Internal factors include strengths (S) and weaknesses (W), which are the resources and experience readily available.

These are some commonly considered internal factors:
- Financial resources, such as funding, sources of revenue;
- Physical resources, such as location, premises, facilities and equipment;
- Human resources including employees, volunteers and target audiences;
- Intellectual property including trademarks, patents and copyrights;
- Current processes including employee programs, department hierarchies and software systems such as CRM software and accounting software.

External Factors

External factors are connected directly or indirectly to an opportunity (O) or a threat (T). They are commonly believed to be uncontrollable by a single company:

- Market trends concerning new products, technological advancements and shifts in target customer needs and preferences;
- Economic trends, such as economic development at local, national and international levels respectively;
- Demographics, especially major demographic changes in target groups;
- Relationships with suppliers and other business partners;
- Political, environmental and economic regulations issued by the authorities.

Questions to Ask

According to Mitchell Weiss, "Companies can't hope to take advantage of or control the external factors until the internals have been objectively assessed." This saying does an excellent job of demystifying the primary objective of SWOT, but how to achieve this aim depends greatly on the questions that you focus during your analysis and planning. The more honest and tougher the questions are, and the more **exhaustive** the process is, the more reliable your analysis will become in making your strategy successful.

The following tough questions are provided for your reference.

Strengths

The strengths of your business should include anything that your business does differently or better than competitors. Think about your unique value proposition, your brand, trends you've noticed in positive customer feedback, operational strengths, and corporate culture. This section is the perfect place to list anything you're already doing well.

Questions to help you determine your strengths:

- What is the unique value proposition of the business?
- What common compliments do you receive from customers?
- How do you operate differently from major competitors?
- What gives you an **edge** on the competition? (better access to raw materials? lower cost of goods? strong corporate culture? high employee morale and motivation?)
- What might your competitors identify as your strengths?

Weaknesses

Your weaknesses are the areas in which the business has room for improvement. You should include structural weaknesses in this section — those that relate to your systems, processes, procedures, resources, and personnel. Common feedback from employees and recurring customer complaints should be listed in this section.

Questions to help you determine your weaknesses:
- What are the common pain points in your customer experience?
- How well do you utilize your resources? Is there any room for improvement?
- What improvements are needed in your employee experience?
- What weaknesses might your customers see that you tend to overlook?
- What weaknesses might your competitors think you have?

Opportunities

Business opportunities are the positive, external factors that one business might benefit from, but cannot directly control. That might include market opportunities, consumer purchasing trends, or gaps of market caused by legal or regulatory changes, demographic changes, etc. For example, businesses that provide accessibility for aging seniors might recognize the forthcoming "silver tsunami" due to longer life expectancy across populations from major economies of the globe. This would be a clear opportunity to expand their customer base.

Questions to help you determine your opportunities:
- What major trends might affect your industry?
- Do your customers ask for anything you don't offer (but could) currently?
- How might demographic changes affect your business opportunities?
- Do your competitors have any weaknesses that could be taken advantage of as opportunities for you?
- Are there any new, or potential, regulatory or tax changes that might provide a new opportunity?

Threats

Your threats are the external factors that have the potential to negatively affect your business. A threat can be specific and competitor-based or more structural. Examples of structural threats could be supply chain challenges, shifts in market requirements, talent shortages, or changes to social media **algorithms** (especially if your business heavily relies on social media marketing).

Questions to help you determine threats:
- What happens if the supply chain is disrupted due to factors such as pandemic or geopolitical conflicts?

- What if a natural disaster (like an earthquake or tsunami) strikes?
- Is your market shrinking? Is it possible that your current business might be replaced by an innovative type of product?
- What technological threats are you typically or potentially vulnerable to (website security, social media algorithm changes)?
- Are you investing enough to meet the rapidly changing technological environment?

On the basis of the results, organizations can determine whether a new project is worth investing or not, and if yes, what additional resources should be allocated or actions would be required to make it successful. An organization's physical, financial and human resources, its processes, past experiences, reputation, competitors, the market movements for the product/service company is offering, the movement of their complimentary and substitute products and other micro-economic and macro-economic factors are all included in this analysis. Upon them, the organizations should come up with recommendations and strategies, which should focus on leveraging strengths and taking advantage of potential opportunities to overcome weaknesses and threats. (1263 words)

(**Source:** https://www.businessnewsdaily.com/4245-swot-analysis.html.)

Vocabulary and Useful Expressions

initiative /ɪˈnɪʃətɪv/	n.	a new plan for dealing with a particular problem or for achieving a particular purpose 倡议，新方案
revamp /ˌriːˈvæmp/	v.	make changes to something in order to try and improve it 修补，修改，改进
landscape /ˈlændskeɪp/	n.	A landscape is all the features that are important in a particular situation. 形势，情形，情状
contingent /kənˈtɪndʒənt/	a.	(formal) depending on sth. that may or may not happen (~ on/upon sth.) 依情况而定的
circumvent /ˌsɜːkəmˈvent/	v.	to find a way of avoiding a difficulty or a rule 设法回避，规避
leverage /ˈlevərɪdʒ/	v.	to use for gain; to exploit; to use (something) to maximum advantage 利用，充分利用

Unit 2 SWOT Analysis

spectrum /ˈspektrəm/	*n.*	a complete or wide range of related qualities, ideas, etc. 范围，各层次	
exhaustive /ɪɡˈzɔːstɪv/	*a.*	including everything possible; very thorough or complete 详尽的，彻底的，全面的	
edge /edʒ/	*n.*	a slight advantage over sb./sth. (~ on/over sb./sth.) （微弱的）优势	
algorithm /ˈælɡərɪðəm/	*n.*	(especially computing) a set of rules that must be followed when solving a particular problem 算法，计算程序	

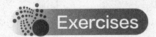

Exercises

Exercise 1. Language: Fill in the blanks with words or expressions from the above article.

1. Currently, the company is under _____ from its main competitors as well as consumers' negative attitude towards cars that burn petrol.
2. In order to realize rapid growth, the company will have to seek for new _____ to expand its business.
3. We need to figure out ways to circumvent _____ and overcome internal _____.
4. To maintain competitive edge, we need to anticipate _____ by closely and carefully monitoring market trends and economic situations.
5. Due to the sudden outbreak of COVID-19 pandemic, the global supplier chain is _____ and impacted the normal operations of companies around the world.
6. The most popular short-video App TikTok changes its _____, which poses a serious challenge to our current social media marketing plan.
7. Considering environmental protection is already a consensus among consumers of the new generation, car manufacturers should seriously take the _____ to develop new car models that are environmentally friendly to cater to this trend.
8. As a company with social conscience, we decided to take _____ examination of our current social marketing practices.
9. It would be wise for the management of the company to make adjustments to its operations _____ upon the results of a series of marketing research.
10. Major _____ changes, such as an increasingly larger market of the senior population, will surely impact on marketing decisions made by the company.

Exercise 2. Knowledge: Work with your partners, and decide which category the following items belong to. Internal factors (S+W) or external factors (O+T)? Write letter I for internal factors, and E for external factors within the brackets.

- intellectual resources ( )
- financial resources ( )
- location ( )
- work efficiency ( )
- product/service price ( )
- management ( )
- infrastructure ( )
- quality of products ( )
- staff qualifications ( )
- staff morale ( )
- transportation ( )
- delivery time ( )
- hours of operations ( )
- distribution channels ( )
- product line ( )
- multiple services ( )
- diversified fields ( )
- sales promotion techniques ( )

- after-sale services ( )
- customer services ( )
- actions of competitors ( )
- fluctuation of interest rates ( )
- exchange rates ( )
- increasing market saturation ( )
- economic conditions ( )
- changes in laws & regulations ( )
- consumer preferences ( )
- political changes ( )
- changes in demographics ( )
- changes in disposable income ( )
- brand image ( )
- leadership ( )
- staff motivation ( )
- corporate culture ( )
- wars ( )
- riots ( )

Exercise 3. Language: Correct the language mistakes you identify in the following sentences.

1. The brand of the company is very strengthened and well-known across the global.

2. An undifferentiated offer will definitely weakness the company's competitiveness in a highly segmented market.

3. Traditional brick-and-mortar retailers are threated by the emerging trend towards online shopping.

4. A gape in the market is often regarded as a market opportunity.

5. The rising environmental awareness of consumers posts a threat to traditional car manufacturers that sell cars with internal combustion engines.

Exercise 4. Knowledge: True or false statements. If the following statements are true, write T; if false, write F.

1. The SWOT analysis mainly deals with analysis of both internal and external factors that may affect or impact a company's business success. ( )
2. External factors are considered outside the company but still controllable. ( )
3. Human resources are considered as part of the external factors. ( )
4. Flexible access to financial resources should be considered as one of the strengths. ( )
5. Changes of algorithms adopted by social media can be regarded as either a threat or opportunity if a company relies on social media marketing. ( )
6. The term silver tsunami refers to the phenomenon that people rush to buy silver as a precious metal to offset fluctuation of foreign exchange rate. ( )
7. Sometimes the weaknesses of competitors can be taken advantage of as opportunities. ( )
8. For a company that mainly provides services for older people, the increasing trend of an ageing population indicates a major opportunity to expand its business. ( )
9. For companies that highly rely on natural resource supplies, natural disasters often spell threats to their normal business operations. ( )
10. In the era of e-commerce, location should be no longer considered as strength. ( )

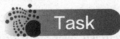

Oral practice: Work with your partners, choose one or two items from Exercise 2, and try to justify (with an example, if possible) why the item belongs to the category of internal factor or external factor. Take turns to report it to each other.

Text C: Extensive Reading

SWOT Analysis of Starbucks

Learning Resources

Starbucks is a globally recognized coffee and beverages brand that has rapidly made strides into almost all major markets of the world. The company has a lead over its principal competitors and other emerging competitors. Indeed, Starbucks is so well known throughout the northern hemisphere that it has become a household name for coffee. Here is a brief analysis of its SWOT factors.

Strengths

- Its strong financial performance has resulted in the company becoming a NO. 1 leader among coffee and beverage retailers in the world.
- The company's market value is about $114 billion (calculated on the basis of its stock price on Jan. 20, 2022), which is a key strength when compared with its competitors.
- The intangible strengths include its top-of-the-mind recall among consumers and by virtue of its brand, which symbolizes excellence and quality at an affordable price.
- The company enjoys a dominant position in the worldwide market for coffee and beverages.
- The company is known for its pioneering people management in an industry where people skills and soft skills make the difference.

Weaknesses

- The company is heavily dependent on its main and key input: the coffee beans. Hence, the price of coffee beans is a key determinant of its profitability. In other words, Starbucks is extremely sensitive to the price fluctuations of coffee beans.
- Many social and environmental activists accused it of the unethical procurement practices when it sources coffee beans from impoverished third-world farmers. Further, the company has also been accused of violating the "Fair Coffee Trade" principles that were put in place a few years ago to tackle this ethical problem.
- The company prices its products in the premium to the middle tiers of the market segment

which places its products outside the budgets of many working consumers who prefer to frequent McDonald's and other outlets for coffee.
- The company must immediately diversify its product range if it has to compete with full-spectrum competitors like McDonald's and Dunkin Donuts in the breakfast segment which is rapidly growing as a consequence of compressed schedules of consumers who would like to grab a bite and drink something instead of making it at home.

Opportunities

- While it may be difficult for a brand like Starbucks to diversify very far from its core products, the company can still broaden its product portfolio, which it has tried in recent years. The company has added snacks and other products to its product portfolio. Diversifying its product portfolio can help the company attract and retain more customers.
- The company has a huge opportunity waiting for it as far as its expansion into the emerging markets is concerned. With a billion consumers likely to join the pool of those who want instant coffee and breakfast in China and India, the company can expand its business in these countries and other emerging markets.
- The focus on digital has grown with the pandemic. While the company has already taken many steps in the past in this direction, it seems Starbucks needs to further adapt its operating model to boost digital sales. Digital marketing will remain a critical driver of sales in the future and therefore requires higher focus by the brand.
- Starbucks also has the opportunity to diversify its delivery system to meet the challenge of the SOHO trend, which encourages employees to work at home. It can expand its business by leveraging the power of Internet, especially mobile Internet to deliver its coffee and other related products more efficiently and effectively to expand its business.
- The company can significantly expand its network of retail stores in the northern hemisphere, as part of its push towards greater market share and more consumer segments.

Threats

- The company faces threats from the rising prices of coffee beans and is subject to supply chain risks related to fluctuations in the prices of this key input. Further, the increase in the prices of dairy products impacts the company adversely leading to another threat to its profitability.
- The company is beset with trademark and copyright infringements from lesser-known rivals who wish to piggyback on its success. As with other multinational retailers in the emerging markets, Starbucks has fought litigation against those misusing its brand and famous logo.
- The company faces intense competition from local coffeehouses and specialty stores that

give the company a run for its money as far as niche consumer segments are concerned. In other words, the company faces a tough challenge from local stores that are patronized by a loyal clientele, which is not enamored of big brands.
- Starbucks has to expand into emerging markets as a necessity as the developed markets that it has traditionally relied on are saturated and given the fact that the ongoing recession has made the going tough for many retailers, it faces significant threats from this aspect.
- Finally, as mentioned earlier, Starbucks faces significant challenges because of its global supply chain and is subject to disruptions in the supply chain because of any reason related to either global or local conditions such as COVID-19 outbreak and geopolitical conflicts. (842 words)

(**Source:** https://www.managementstudyguide.com/swot-analysis-of-starbucks.htm.)

Writing: Select a company or a brand that you are familiar with, search for its information online, and try to conduct a general SWOT analysis of it. Write a brief report on the basis of your research.

As for the format of the report, you can refer to the "SWOT Analysis of Starbucks" mentioned above. You are expected and encouraged to use both the language and knowledge learned in this unit.

Word limit: 300 words.

Unit 3

Marketing Strategy

🔔 *Quote of the Unit:*

"Today it's important to be present, be relevant and add value."
—Nick Besbeas, former CMO of LinkedIn

🔔 *Learning Objectives:*

1. Understand essential concepts and terms of marketing strategy.
2. Understand the language used in discussing marketing strategy issues.
3. Apply both the language and knowledge learned to describing the marketing strategy of a company.

🔔 *Pre-class Questions:*

1. How do you understand the importance of devising an appropriate marketing strategy for a business?
2. Do you know what are the major components of a marketing strategy for a business?
3. Do you know some commonly adopted marketing strategies?

Text A: Lead-in

Learning Resources

The Success of Patagonia's Marketing Strategy

By Poonkulali Thangavelu

Patagonia, a manufacturer of **upscale** outdoor clothing and **gears**, is known for various environmental sustainability efforts. The privately held company has adopted a unique marketing strategy promoting used wear and asking consumers to think twice before buying its products. In spite of what looks like an anti-marketing effort, the company has actually seen its revenues grow in the last few years — despite the recession.

How has the company managed to make this happen?

"Don't Buy This Jacket" Campaign

With consumers becoming more frugal during the recession and its aftermath, they were less inclined to buy on **impulse** and tended to shop more for value. They were interested in goods that lasted long, and Patagonia saw an opportunity there to tout its own long-lasting wares. That led to the company's running an advertisement during the 2011 Thanksgiving season that read "Don't Buy This Jacket." The advertisement talked about the cost to the environment of one of the company's best-selling fleece sweaters and asked consumers to reconsider before buying the product and instead opt for a used Patagonia product. In spite of this, or because of this, the company saw its revenues grow about 30 percent to $543 million in 2012, followed by another six percent growth in 2013.

Walking the Walk

What resonates with Patagonia customers is that the company doesn't just talk the environmental talk. Patagonia founder Yvon Chouinard also backs up the company's talk with its actions. The company donates a portion of its revenue to environmental causes and uses recycled, "Fair Trade" certified, and organic material in its clothing. It also uses solar energy at its company headquarters, and it is one of the founders of the **Sustainable** Apparel Coalition, a group of companies that promise to reduce their environmental footprint.

Patagonia has also engaged in initiatives such as sending out an environmentally friendly truck on a trip across the country, in a bid to help consumers repair their outdoor gear and sell used Patagonia wares to them. Moreover, as a way to promote used Patagonia wear, the company has invested in Yerdle, a **startup** that aims to cut down on peoples' purchases of new products. And another Patagonia advertisement campaign in 2013 warned against the sort of development that used up the earth's resources.

Resonates with Target Audience

It seems that the company's message has resonated with the sort of environmentally conscious and upscale consumers that Patagonia sees as its target audience. These sorts of consumers like the idea of buying a product that is made by an environmentally friendly company in an environmentally friendly manner. Beyond lasting a long time, the products can also be recycled for further use. As the company has tapped into more consumers in this target market, they have managed to expand their sales. And the company's consumers could also have taken advantage of its efforts to **facilitate** the sale of used products and have used the money to buy new Patagonia products.

Of course, it is likely that others who were not so environmentally conscious just bought the product after seeing the company's advertisements. It also doesn't appear that everyone is religiously following the company's **exhortation** to recycle; the company only recycles a minor portion of its annual sales.

Nonetheless, as a result of its successful marketing, Patagonia has opened 40 stores globally since 2011, another factor that could be behind its sales growth. The company has also launched an environmentally friendly food business.

The Bottom Line

Even as Patagonia has led an effort to expand the useful life of its products, an effort that is **at odds** with the planned **obsolescence** approach of many manufacturers today, it has seen its sales rise. It seems the company's environmentally friendly efforts have resonated with the sort of consumer it targets. More of these people are buying Patagonia products as they see the company's long-lasting wares as a way to express their values. (663 words)

(**Source:** https://www.investopedia.com/articles/personal-finance/070715/success-patagonias-marketing-strategy.asp#ixzz56cs1JFZ8.)

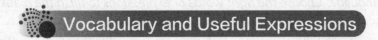

Vocabulary and Useful Expressions

upscale /ˌʌpˈskeɪl/	*a.*	Upscale is used to describe products or services that are expensive, of good quality, and intended to appeal to people in a high social class. （产品或服务）高档的，质优价高的
gear /ɡɪə(r)/	*n.*	the gear involved in a particular activity is the equipment or special clothing that you use （某一特定活动的）设备，服装
impulse /ˈɪmpʌls/	*n.*	a sudden strong wish or need to do sth., without stopping to think about the results (~ to do sth.) 冲动，心血来潮，一时的念头
sustainable /səˈsteɪnəbl/	*a.*	involving the use of natural products and energy in a way that does not harm the environment 不破坏生态平衡的，合理利用的
startup /ˈstɑːtʌp/	*n.*	a company that has been newly established for business 初创公司
resonate /ˈrezəneɪt/	*v.*	to remind sb. of sth.; to be similar to what sb. thinks or believes (~ with sb./sth.) 使产生联想，引起共鸣
facilitate /fəˈsɪlɪteɪt/	*v.*	(formal) to make an action or a process possible or easier 促进，促使，使便利
exhortation /ˌeɡzɔːˈteɪʃn/	*n.*	the act of exhorting; an earnest attempt at persuasion 规劝，敦促，告诫
at odds		to disagree with sb. about sth. (be ~ with sb.; be ~ over/on sth.) （就某事）（与某人）有分歧
obsolescence /ˌɒbsəˈlesns/	*n.*	(formal) the state of becoming old-fashioned and no longer useful (= becoming obsolete) 过时，陈旧，淘汰

Exercise 1. Language: Choose the right words or expressions to fill in the blanks.

| resonate | startup | gear | impulsive | exhortation |
| sustainable | obsolescence | upscale | facilitate | at odds |

1. _____ buying is the sudden and immediate purchase of a product without any intention of buying prior to the shopping experience.
2. Products with planned _____ are intentionally designed not to last long so that people will have to buy new ones.
3. A _____ is a venture that is initiated recently by its founders around an idea or a problem with a potential for significant business opportunity and impact.
4. Starbucks has successfully acquired a/an _____ image among the middle-income city dwellers in China.
5. The creation of an efficient and _____ transport system is critical to the future development of Guangzhou city as a metropolis.
6. I'm curious how can a brand _____ with its target audience meaningfully?
7. The new international airport has _____ the development local tourism greatly since its inception.
8. These findings of the current market research seem to be _____ with what is going on in the FMCG market.
9. Despite _____ to stay away from Bitcoin, many investors still rush in.
10. I used to wear trendy _____ , but it just looked ridiculous on me.

Exercise 2. Knowledge: Read the article again and try to identify the major characteristics of Patagonia's target customers. Report it orally to your partners and justify.

Exercise 3. Knowledge: Read the article again and try to find out the positioning of Patagonia in the market. Report it orally to your partners and justify.

Exercise 4. Knowledge: Read the article again and try to find out the marketing objectives of Patagonia. Report it orally to your partners and justify.

Exercise 5. Knowledge: Read the article again and try to summarize the secret to Patagonia's success. Report it orally to your partners and justify.

Text B: Intensive Reading

Definition & Overview of Marketing Strategy

Learning Resources

A marketing strategy is generally regarded as the overall **game plan** for reaching **prospective** consumers and **converting** them into customers. It is also the marketing logic by which the company creates and delivers value for customers, achieves long-term mutually beneficial customer relationships.

Before **formulating** a decent and effective marketing strategy, the company should conduct a careful marketing research and decide which group of consumers (target market) it will serve (by way of market **segmentation** and targeting) and how it will serve (by way of differentiation and positioning).

A decent marketing strategy should cover the 4Ps of marketing — product, price, place, and promotion. They are very essential in shaping the crucial strategies to boost sales and generate profits for the company:
- Product strategies
- Pricing strategies
- Distribution strategies
- Promotion strategies

Why Your Business Needs a Marketing Strategy

You may wonder why your business still needs a marketing strategy, given that you already have a marketing plan, marketing management, marketing objectives, and goals. Here are some simple reasons:

Firstly, a decent marketing strategy provides a blueprint or roadmap for achieving the objectives of the business. Secondly, as mentioned above, the formulation of a marketing strategy requires detailed market research, thus it can help improve a company's overall understanding of the environment in which it operates, providing valuable **insight** into the company's target segment, better enabling decision makers to cater to their customers' needs. Thirdly, a clear and effective marketing strategy enables a more efficient allocation and use of the company's resources by identifying areas in greater need of improvement, such as customer acquisition and retention. Finally, it can point out cohesive direction for all stakeholders of the company, improving inter-departmental co-ordination and reducing duplication of efforts.

How to Develop an Effective Marketing Strategy

For developing an effective marketing strategy, it is necessary to know your competitors and know that your offering boasts added-value that your competitors do not have (FAB analysis- features, advantages and benefits).

After this define your target market in a demographic and **psychographic** way, this will help you understand why they need to buy products/services from you.

There are several ways to make marketing strategies effective, so it is necessary to focus on the most important communication channels (traditional vs. social media) and to be able to carry out the strategies with a successful follow-up of the implementation.

Establish the Objectives and the Process

- Analyze your position in the market: identify the target audience, the market competition and what is happening in the company. In addition, define which are the strong aspects and those that you should optimize.
- Establish goals: create achievable brand and sales objectives and determine the time frame to reach them (by way of setting SMART goals).
- Design the tactics: after you examine the landscape, create the lines of action based on the strategies.
- Implement controls: define how you will measure goal achievement and how you expect performance to improve.

Marketing Strategy vs. Marketing Plan

An effective marketing strategy consists of all the efforts that a company does to achieve its business goals.

Marketing plan, on the other hand, is formulated to help achieve the company's marketing goals. A marketing plan provides detailed **operational** guidelines on how to move from one point to another.

To put it simple, we can say that marketing strategy tells you "where to go" (directional) and "what to do", marketing plan explains "how to do it" (operational). Some people make mistakes when they start with "how to do it" without defining the first "where" and "what" questions.

The following is an example that tries to illustrate the relationship between marketing strategy and marketing plan.

- *Objective*: To achieve a higher market share.
- *Marketing strategy*: Enter a new market segment.
- *Marketing plan*: Develop a marketing campaign that reaches, identifies and focuses on the specific market segment.

The following are some commonly adopted marketing strategies.

Undifferentiated or Mass Marketing

Under this strategy the marketer attempts to appeal to one large market with a single marketing strategy. While this approach offers advantages in terms of lowering development and production costs, since only one product is marketed, there are few markets in which all customers seek the same benefits. While this approach was very popular in the early days of marketing (e.g., Ford Model-T car, introduced to the world in 1908), few companies now view this as a feasible strategy.

Differentiated or Segmentation Marketing

Marketers that adopt this strategy normally try to appeal to multiple smaller markets with a unique marketing strategy for each. The underlying concept is that bigger markets can be divided into many sub-markets and an organization chooses different marketing strategies to reach each sub-market it targets. Most large consumer product firms follow this strategy as they offer multiple products (e.g., jogging shoes, running shoes, basketball shoes, badminton shoes) within a larger product category (e.g., footwear).

Concentrated or Niche Marketing

This strategy combines mass and segmentation marketing by using a single marketing strategy to appeal to one or more very small markets (as niches). It is primarily used by smaller marketers who have identified small sub-segments of a larger segment that are not well served by larger firms that follow a segmentation marketing approach. In these situations a smaller company can do quite well marketing a single product to a narrowly defined target market.

Customized or Micro-marketing

This target marketing strategy attempts to appeal to targeted customers with individualized marketing programs. For micro-marketing segmentation to be effective the marketer must, to some degree, allow customers to "build" their own products. This approach requires extensive technical capability for marketers to reach individual customers and allow customers to interact with the marketer. The Internet has been the **catalyst** for this target marketing strategy. This is also called mass-customization. As more companies utilize the Internet in a more profound manner, micro-marketing is expected to **flourish**. (974 words)

Vocabulary and Useful Expressions

game plan		a plan for success in the future, especially in sport, politics or business （尤指体育运动、政治或商业方面的）行动计划，方案，对策
prospective /prəˈspektɪv/	a.	expected to do sth. or to become sth. 有望的，可能成为的，预期的，潜在的
convert /kənˈvɜːt/	v.	to change to a new religion, belief, opinion, etc., or to make someone do this （使人）转变为/转化为
formulate /ˈfɔːmjuleɪt/	v.	to create or prepare sth. carefully, giving particular attention to the details 制订，规划，构想，准备
segmentation /ˌsegmenˈteɪʃn/	n.	(technical) the act of dividing sth. into different parts; one of these parts （术语）分割，细分
insight /ˈɪnsaɪt/	n.	an accurate and deep understanding of a complex situation or problem （对复杂形势或问题的）洞察，深入见解
psychographic /ˌsaɪkəʊˈɡræfɪk/	a.	concerning the study of customers in relation to their opinions, interests, and emotions （有关）消费者心理特征的
operational /ˌɒpəˈreɪʃənl/	a.	connected with the way in which a business, machine, system, etc. works 操作的，运转的，运营的，业务的
undifferentiated /ˈʌnˌdɪfəˈrenʃɪeɪtɪd/	a.	having parts that you cannot distinguish between; not split into different parts or sections 无法区分的，分不开的，一体的
catalyst /ˈkætəlɪst/	n.	a person or thing that causes a change (~ for sth.) 促使变化的人，引发变化的因素
flourish /ˈflʌrɪʃ/	v.	to develop quickly and be successful or common 繁荣，昌盛，兴旺

Unit 3 Marketing Strategy

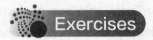

Exercise 1. Language: Correct the language mistakes you identify in the following sentences.

1. A marketing strategy is generally regarded as the overall game plan for reach prospective consumers and convert them into customers.

2. The company should conducted a careful marketing research and decide which group of consumers it will serve.

3. Marketing plan, on the other hand, is form to help achieve the company's marketing goals.

4. While this approach was very popularity in the early days of marketing, few companies now view this as a feasibility strategy.

5. Under this strategy the marketer attempts to appear to one large market with a single marketing strategy.

Exercise 2. Knowledge: True or false statements. If the following statements are true, write T; if false, write F.

1. Undifferentiated marketing strategy used to be popular in the early days of marketing, boasting benefits such as lower development costs and production costs, bringing more benefits to customers who had few choices. ( )

2. It should be regarded as a marketing strategy if the marketer develops a marketing campaign that reaches, identifies and focuses on the specific market segment. ( )

3. A marketing strategy normally provides answers to questions like where should the company go, how should it perform to achieve its marketing objectives. ( )

4. A company earns profits by way of creating and delivering values to target customers. ( )

5. Thanks to the rapid development of Internet and IT, customized marketing now allows,

to some degree, customers to "build" their own products. ( )
6. A marketing plan provides detailed directional guidelines on how to move from one point to another. ( )
7. Most large consumer product firms follow undifferentiated marketing strategy as they offer multiple products within a larger product category. ( )
8. If a small company adopts niche marketing, it will concentrate all its marketing efforts to serve a specific small market segment well. ( )
9. The formulation of a marketing strategy requires detailed market research, thus it can help improve a company's overall insight into the marketing environment in which it operates. ( )
10. An effective marketing strategy enables a company to better allocate its resources to areas that are in greater need of input. ( )

Exercise 3. Language: Fill in the blanks with words or expressions from the above article.

1. Marketers that adopt this strategy normally try to _____ to multiple smaller markets with a unique marketing strategy for each.
2. A thorough marketing research can provide valuable _____ into the company's target segment.
3. I sincerely hope that this case will prove to be a _____ for a major change in the market.
4. It is an imperative task for the marketers to attract prospective consumers and make efforts to _____ into real customers.
5. The marketing plan provides an _____ instruction on how to achieve marketing objectives.
6. Demographic data takes into account broad areas of a target audience like age, race, and income. _____ data compiles opinions and interests from the target market.
7. Business goals and marketing are _____ to each other, considering that an effective marketing strategy consists of all the efforts that a company does to achieve its business goals.
8. It is universally acknowledged that few businesses can _____ in economic recessions.
9. In that case, some scholars brought forward a new production mode — mass _____ in 1987.
10. Market _____ is a process that consists of sectioning the target market into smaller groups that share similar characteristics.

Unit 3 Marketing Strategy

Oral practice: It is mentioned in the first sentence that the purpose of the marketing strategy is to reach prospective consumers and convert them into customers. Then do you know what are the differences between the two terms consumer and customer? Discuss and justify.

Text C: Extensive Reading

Learning Resources

Marketing Strategy of Starbucks

From a functional perspective, marketing strategy is formed by the strategies of the marketing mix or the 4Ps of marketing which are absolutely variables of great importance to achieving commercial objectives. Starbucks has adopted several marketing strategies like product innovation, pricing approach, promotion planning, etc. These strategies, based on Starbucks marketing mix, help the brand succeed.

Product Strategy

Starbucks is a leading coffee chain brand with wide and deep global presence. With its commitment to product innovation, it provides an unbeatable and unrivalled experience for the various coffee products it offers. Although Starbucks' speciality is coffee, it has entered  various other product categories to extend its business by attracting more customers.

Starbucks outlets serve whole bean coffee, hot and cold drinks, instant micro-ground coffee known as VIA, whole-bean coffee, Caffè Latte, La Boulange pastries, espresso, full-leaf and loose-leave teas like Teavana tea products, Frappuccino beverages, Evolution Fresh juices and snacks such as chips and crackers; seasonal or specific to store locality products like Pumpkin Spice Latte.

The coffees are categorized on the basis of:

45

- Format — whole bean and VIA instant coffee;
- Roast — blonde, medium, dark;
- Caffeine — regular, decaf;
- Flavored and unflavored.

Price/Pricing Strategy

Starbucks is clearly a premium priced coffee seller.

The price is justified due to its high end technology and the varieties it offers along with the best customer experience. To maintain competition, Starbucks started with a low cost range at few outlets and to cater the customers who couldn't be attracted by its high prices. The packaged products are also available at grocery stores which are comparatively less expensive than the normal outlet products and easily available to everyone. This proves that Starbucks not only follows competitive pricing in its marketing mix but also relative pricing strategies.

The drinks at Starbucks are also available in various sizes as per the need and requirement of every customer with minute variations like *demi, short, mini, tall, grande, venti* and *trenta* (all expressed in Italian). The quality is always the highest, which helps maintain a loyal customer base and a quality brand name. The price is generally high because the focus is not only to provide high quality coffee, but its ambience and experience which is of high value.

Place & Distribution Strategy

Starbucks has prominent global presence. As of November 2021, the company had 33,833 stores in 80 countries, 15,444 of which were located in the United States. Out of Starbucks' U.S.-based stores, over 8,900 are company-operated, while the remainder are licensed.

Starbucks have a well-designed website with very succinct layout, providing navigation buttons for its menu, rewards and gift cards sections. The complete Starbucks menu, store options, locations, speciality stores, customer perks and benefits, can be found by clicking these buttons respectively. If visitors want to find a nearby local Starbucks store, they can click the button labeled "find a store". They also provide a mobile App for smartphone users, which allows them to make an order on-the-go. With the growth of e-commerce and online-to-offline deliveries, the brand has managed to increase its reach and sales. If customers want to know more about coffee making, coffee varieties available, sourcing options, they can search the website for more information.

Promotion & Advertising Strategy

Starbucks is a top-of-the-mind brand through various activities and initiatives. Starbucks focuses on brand promotion in its marketing mix through channels like online advertisement, TV commercials, print advertisements, etc. Even though Starbucks has a wide range of customer network, it never falls back from its responsibility towards its customers: benefits are offered for the price they pay and given back to the society. It adopts social marketing strategies by way of ethical sourcing options providing benefits to farmers in coffee, tea and cocoa sourcing areas. It also adopts environment friendly techniques, recyclable cups, green building, etc. to clearly displays the responsibilities and actions taken by the company. Apart from this, Starbucks makes good use of technology for promotions like the "tweet-a-coffee" campaign, loyalty program and gift cards with free in-store WiFi, zero charges for selected coffee and milk options, etc. to increase customer loyalty and thus retain them.

If you are interested in this company, you are recommended to simply go online and search for more information about Starbucks.　(710 words)

Writing: Select a company or a brand that you are familiar with, search for its information online, and try to conduct a general marketing strategy analysis of it. You can refer to the article above for format.

Word limit: 500 words.

Unit 4

Marketing Ethics

Quote of the Unit:

"Quality means doing it right when no one is looking."

—Henry Ford

Learning Objectives:

1. Understand the basic concepts and terms of marketing ethics.
2. Understand the various forms of marketing ethics embodiment.
3. Apply the language and knowledge learned in this unit to describe and discuss issues related to marketing ethics.

Pre-class Questions:

1. Have you ever heard of the term ethics? If yes, what does it mean to you?
2. What does it mean to be ethical in marketing? Why do marketers need to behave in an ethical way when it comes to marketing?
3. What ethical issues may be related to marketing?

Text A: Lead-in

Ethical Marketing: the Example of a Conscientious Company

Adapted from Dan Shewan

Learning Resources

A recent AFLAC survey, which mainly investigated the potential business impact of ethical commerce and corporate **philanthropy**, revealed that 92% of Millennial consumers are more likely to buy products from ethical companies, and 82% of them believe ethical brands **outperform** similar companies that lack a commitment to ethical principles.

Brand **authenticity** has never been more crucial to the success of one business, and companies that have **dedicated** themselves to the greater **good** instead of solely sticking to their bottom lines have witnessed a remarkable surge in both support and revenue.

What Is Ethical Marketing?

Ethical marketing refers to the process by which companies market their goods and services by focusing not only on how their products can benefit customers, but also how they can benefit socially responsible or environmental **causes**.

Image via World Fair Trade Organization

To put this another way, ethical marketing isn't a strategy; it's a philosophy. It includes everything from ensuring advertisements are honest and trustworthy, to building strong relationships with consumers through a set of shared values. Companies with a focus on ethical marketing evaluate their decisions from a business perspective (i.e. whether a particular marketing initiative will deliver the desired return) as well as a moral perspective (i.e. whether a decision is "right" or morally sound).

Ethical Marketing Example: TOMS

Many ladies love TOMS ballet flats. They're cute, comfortable, and best of all, socially conscious.

TOMS isn't just engaged in corporate philanthropy to make a quick buck; it's a core part of the company's values.

TOMS was founded by Blake Mycoskie in 2006 following a trip to Argentina. During his visit, Mycoskie saw first-hand how people living in impoverished areas of Argentina had to live without shoes, a challenge that many of us likely give little thought. Inspired by his trip, Mycoskie decided to establish his company with giving in mind.

Since 2006, TOMS' footwear business has donated more than 60 million pairs of shoes to children in need all over the world. As if that weren't enough, TOMS' eyewear division has given more than 400,000 pairs of glasses to visually impaired people who lack access to eye care.

The company has further diversified its operations to include clean water initiatives through its coffee business, and its line of bags has helped support projects to expand access to birthing kits to expectant mothers in developing nations as well as training for birth attendants. To date, TOMS has helped more than 25,000 women safely deliver their babies.

How Does TOMS Use Ethical Marketing?

TOMS puts its social and environmental philanthropy on full display in virtually every aspect of its branding. This not only lets potential customers know the kind of company they're dealing with right off the bat, but also reinforces TOMS' brand values consistently across all channels.

Take a look at TOMS' homepage. Right underneath the carousel, the company tells you that, for every product you purchase, TOMS will help someone in need.

TOMS' mission is so central to the company's branding, it's given almost equal emphasis on its website as the products it sells. In fact, it's almost impossible to navigate through TOMS' website without seeing further examples of how TOMS helps people around the world.

This isn't a typically **cynical** attempt to **capitalize on** empty gestures or a feel-good sales tactic; it's the same principle leveraged by brands that use display advertising. Just as many display ads are designed to promote brand awareness and achieve top-of-mind presence among consumers, TOMS' philanthropic mission is constantly reinforced throughout its website and marketing materials. As a result, it's almost impossible to think of TOMS as a brand without thinking of the company's various **outreach** projects and corporate giving initiatives.   (622 words)

Vocabulary and Useful Expressions

philanthropy /fɪˈlænθrəpɪ/	n.	the practice of helping the poor and those in need, especially by giving money 博爱，慈善，乐善好施
outperform /ˌaʊtpəˈfɔːm/	v.	to achieve better results than sb./sth. （效益上）超过，胜过
authenticity /ˌɔːθenˈtɪsətɪ/	n.	the quality of being genuine or true 真实性，确实性
dedicate /ˈdedɪkeɪt/	v.	to give a lot of your time and effort to a particular activity or purpose because you think it is important 把……奉献给
good /ɡʊd/	n.	something that helps sb./sth. 用处，好处，益处
cause /kɔːz/	n.	an organization or idea that people support or fight for （支持或为之奋斗的）事业，目标，思想
cynical /ˈsɪnɪkl/	a.	not caring that sth. might hurt other people, if there is some advantage for you 只顾自己不顾他人的，见利忘义的
capitalize on		to gain a further advantage for yourself from a situation 充分利用，从……中获得更多的好处
outreach /ˈaʊtriːtʃ/	n.	the activity of an organization that provides a service or advice to people in the community, especially those who cannot or are unlikely to come to an office, a hospital, etc. for help 外展服务（在服务机构以外的场所提供的社区服务等）

Exercises

Exercise 1. Language: Translate the following sentences into Chinese.

1. TOMS isn't just engaged in corporate philanthropy to make a quick buck; it's a core part of the company's values and brand.

2. It includes everything from ensuring advertisements are honest and trustworthy, to building strong relationships with consumers through a set of shared values.

3. TOMS' philanthropic mission is constantly reinforced throughout its website and marketing materials.

4. It's almost impossible to navigate through TOMS' website without seeing further examples of how TOMS helps people around the world.

5. This isn't a typically cynical attempt to capitalize on empty gestures or a feel-good sales tactic.

Exercise 2. Knowledge: True or false statements. If the following statements are true, write T; if false, write F.

1. Ethical marketing should be regarded as a strategy and a philosophy.   (   )
2. Brand authenticity has never been crucial to the success of one business in the past years.   (   )
3. Companies that adopt corporate philanthropy as a quick way to earn profits.   (   )
4. Ethical marketing depends on a long-term continuing education, campaigning, etc. to encourage and help people make more conscious buying decisions.   (   )
5. TOMS donated birthing kits to mothers delivering babies and provide training for birth attendants in developing countries.   (   )
6. TOMS has adopted ethical marketing not as an easy method that they can take advantage of to increase sales.   (   )

7. TOMS does not only practice ethical marketing but also present its good deeds on its website and other channels to convey these messages. (   )
8. Footwear, bags and eyewear are included in the categories of products offered by TOMS. (   )
9. Companies can find out the benefits of focusing on both profits (from a business perspective) and people (from a moral perspective). (   )
10. Companies can practice ethical marketing by dedicating to philanthropic causes. (   )

Oral practice: Work with your partners. As one of the Millennial consumers, is it true that you prefer products or brands of companies that are engaged in ethical marketing? If the answer is yes, can you use one example to justify it? If the answer is no, what factors of a product or a brand may appeal to you more? Discuss and report it.

Text B: Intensive Reading

Marketing Ethics

Learning Resources

In the term "marketing ethics", the word "ethics" refers to a system of moral principles or moral codes governing the appropriate conducts for a person or a group. In other words, ethics tell people the proper ways to behave and what conducts should be avoided.

Business ethics is one of the most complicated and **contentious** subjects in human history. The relationship between doing the right things and making money has been studied by both **academics** and business leaders for years with little **consensus** reached.

In reality, there is one fact that people tend to appreciate those who can insist on conducting ethically, doing what is right, protecting the values that they hold true. The same applies to businesses. If one business insists on doing business in an ethical way that would very much promote its corporate image, attracting more consumers who align themselves with the company's values, and tend to buy more from those companies with positive images.

Therefore, companies realize the importance of acting in more ethical ways and conveying this message to their target customers. One of the easiest ways to achieve this is through their marketing practices.

For companies seeking to improve the image of a brand and develop long-term relationships with customers, ethical marketing is a way that one must go through. Customers do not want to feel **manipulated** by the brands they like. Companies can use ethical marketing as a way to develop a sense of trust among their customers.

If a product lives up to the claims it made in advertisement, it reflects positively on the entire company. In modern business world, more and more companies do not only pursue profits without considering their corporate image in the eyes of customers, but also allocate some resources to perform their corporate social responsibilities.

For example, they start to follow the practices of social marketing, cause-related marketing, green marketing, responsible purchasing, etc. These marketing practices can help build a decent and positive corporate image for companies, thus would help enhance and strengthen the ties between them and consumers.

And now let's explore them one by one.

First, social marketing. Social marketing refers to the act of using marketing techniques to convince people to change their behaviors for their own good or for the benefit of the society as a whole. For example, some companies or organizations may use TV **commercials** to ask people to eat less red meat and eat more white meat in order to stay healthy.

The goal of social marketing is to minimize social problems such as negative behaviors, crime or poverty.

In China, a famous former basketball player Yao Ming and other **celebrities** cooperated with one charity organization to put on TV advertisement asking people to refuse to eat shark's fin just to save this precious sea animal since Chinese people regard shark's fin as one precious and nutritious food and eat a lot every year, causing deaths of many sharks.

In order to impress the audience, the advertisement used slogan like this "No trading, no killing". This social marketing campaign was quite successful and people started to use this slogan in their daily lives. The charity organization who initiated this campaign won a lot of attention and became famous.

The second practice is called cause-related marketing. A good cause means something or somebody deserving help, especially a charity. When a company donates money to a charity, a non-profit organization or a good cause, then the brand is associated with the charity. This association will surely help build up a positive brand image. The company's partnership with a charity or non-profit organization is surely mutually beneficial.

For the good cause, it can get more necessary resources to fund its activities or campaigns such as poverty alleviation projects. At the same time the company will enjoy better corporate image. Generally, the good cause requires potential corporate partner to share its principles and values.

Third, green marketing. Green marketing is the development and distribution of products that are presumed to be environmentally safe, eco-friendly. It incorporates a broad range of activities including product modification, changes to the production process, sustainable packaging, as well as modifying advertising. For example, some washing powder producers **hail** their products as being not harmful to the environment. This phenomenon is quite commonly seen in many industries these days.

Refrigerator manufacturers often stress that the chemical used to cool down is no longer harmful to the atmosphere. Agricultural producers keep mentioning that they do not use chemical fertilizers nor agrochemical. They use this rhetoric to advertise, hoping to establish a so-called green image for their products.

The last one, responsible purchasing. Responsible purchasing is another way that a company can build or maintain good reputation among its customers. Responsible purchasing is a practice which is dedicated to socially responsible and environmentally sustainable purchasing. They are expected to use **cutting-edge procurement** tools and resources designed to save money, conserve resources, reduce waste, and improve efficiency.

In this sense, companies should refuse to buy materials or goods made using child labor or that have been tested on animals. The former shows a concern for human rights, the latter concerns about animal testing.

One company that embodies this spirit is the Body Shop, a worldwide chain of bath and body stores. Since its inception it has been committed to treating workers fairly, avoiding animal testing, using organic products and promoting healthy body images.

These values are often at the center of their marketing efforts. The ethical nature of the company is highlighted as a way to differentiate themselves from their competitors in the cosmetics industry.

Hence, in order to improve the company's fame, it formulated and implemented a policy of sustainable purchasing or sourcing only allowing to buy raw materials, products that come from **renewable** sources and legal manufacturers. In this sense, the company maintains high level of moral standards.

To sum up, marketing ethics refer to the moral codes governing a company's conducts in promoting its product and brand image. Practices such as social marketing, cause-related marketing, green marketing, responsible purchasing are widely used to help establish positive corporate image and win more customers. Maintaining high ethical standards in practicing marketing hence is a beneficial way to a company's sustainable development.　　(1041 words)

Vocabulary and Useful Expressions

contentious	/kənˈtenʃəs/	a.	likely to cause disagreement between people 可能引起争论的
academic	/ˌækəˈdemɪk/	n.	scholar in university 学者
consensus	/kənˈsensəs/	n.	an opinion that all members of a group agree with 一致的意见，共识
manipulate	/məˈnɪpjuleɪt/	v.	(disapproving) to control or influence sb./sth., often in a dishonest way so that they do not realize it （暗中）控制，操纵，影响
commercial	/kəˈmɜːʃl/	n.	an advertisement on the radio or on television （电台或电视播放的）广告
celebrity	/səˈlebrətɪ/	n.	someone who is famous, especially in areas of entertainment such as films, music, writing, or sport 名人，明星
hail	/heɪl/	v.	to describe sb./sth. as being very good or special, especially in newspapers, etc. 赞扬（或称颂）……为……（尤用于报纸等）
cutting-edge	/ˌkʌtɪŋˈedʒ/	a.	in accord with the most fashionable ideas or style 最前沿的，尖端的
procurement	/prəˈkjuəmənt/	n.	the process of obtaining supplies of sth., especially for a government or an organization （尤指为政府或机构）采购，购买
renewable	/rɪˈnjuːəbl/	a.	that is replaced naturally or controlled carefully and can therefore be used without the risk of finishing it all 可更新的，可再生的，可恢复的

Unit 4   Marketing Ethics

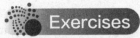 Exercises

Exercise 1. Language: Fill in the blanks with words of expressions from the above article.

1. The word "ethics" refers to a system of moral _____ or moral _____ governing the appropriate conducts for a person or a group.
2. They start to follow the practices of social marketing, _____ -related marketing and green marketing.
3. By adopting ethical marketing practices, companies can _____ and _____ a positive relationship with customers.
4. Social marketing refers to the act of using marketing techniques to convince people to change their _____.
5. When a company donates money or cooperate with a good cause, the company's name is then _____ with the charity.
6. Companies that practice green marketing are believed to be providing goods that are environmentally _____ and _____.
7. Refrigerator and air-conditioner manufacturers often hail that the chemical used to cool down is no longer _____ to the _____.
8. The ethical nature of the company is highlighted as a way to _____ themselves from their competitors in the industry.
9. Responsible purchasing is a practice which is dedicated to socially _____ and environmentally _____ purchasing.
10. One example of responsible purchasing is the introduction of a regulation that only allows buying raw materials, products that come from _____ sources and _____ manufacturers.

Exercise 2. Knowledge: True or false statements. If the following statements are true, write T; if false, write F.

1. Responsible purchasing refers to the practice that the purchaser of the raw materials or other component parts should be responsible for the company's business success such as high profitability. ( )
2. The goals of social marketing include encouraging people to change their negative behaviors and to persuade people not to commit crimes. ( )
3. It seems social marketing advertisements featuring celebrities are effective. ( )
4. It is mutually beneficial for a company to cooperate with a charity or a non-profit organization to promote socially responsible projects. ( )
5. Better corporate image is also one major factor that drives companies to commit to

59

ethical marketing. ( )
6. In modern business world, companies tend to pay more attention to erecting a good corporate image besides the sheer pursuit of profits. ( )
7. Maintaining high ethical standards in terms of marketing is an effective and beneficial way to realize a company's sustainable development. ( )
8. Customers tend to align themselves with companies sharing core values with them. ( )
9. Being ethical and profitable at the same time is almost impossible for marketers. ( )
10. Acting sincerely in an ethical way instead of resorting to untrue hype to promote one's products will generate good results in the long term. ( )

Exercise 3. Language: Match the words from Column A with those from Column B.

Column A	Column B
1. socially	A. sustainable
2. good	B. cause
3. moral	C. principles
4. corporate	D. responsible
5. appropriate	E. image
6. production	F. conducts
7. contentious	G. process
8. hold	H. subject
9. conserve	I. true
10. environmentally	J. resource

Oral practice: Work with your partners. Choose one company that you are familiar with, and think about what it has done in terms of ethical marketing. Point out which category does it fall into, social marketing, cause-related marketing, green marketing, or responsible purchasing. What are the possible benefits according to your observation or past experience? Share your ideas, and you are encouraged to use both the language and knowledge learned in this unit.

Text C: Extensive Reading

Learning Resources

Driving Balanced Development[①]

According to the ITU (International Telecommunication Union), nearly half of the world's population is not yet connected to the Internet. Most of them live in underdeveloped rural areas and make their living from the land. Although they are living in the digital age, they cannot benefit from digital technology and the opportunities it provides. Huawei's TECH4ALL digital inclusion initiative helps rural areas and underdeveloped industries in developing countries to develop using ICT. We are committed to providing low-cost ICT infrastructure in remote areas, and taking targeted actions to remove the obstacles to last-mile Internet access. With our digital technologies, we help industries go digital and smart so that they will not fall behind. We also help improve working conditions for people who do heavy, repetitive, and dangerous work, so that they can work more safely, more efficiently, and with more dignity.

RuralStar: Remote Doesn't Mean Unconnected

Many remote areas in Africa are described as information deserts, because a lack of telecommunications infrastructure means the people living there are unable to make phone calls or access the Internet. These remote areas tend to have low population densities, unstable power supplies, and poor road conditions. Deploying traditional cell towers would be difficult and expensive. To address the communication gaps in these areas, Huawei carefully studied local conditions and created an innovative base station which can be installed on just a wooden pole. It is called RuralStar. It is compact and powered by solar energy and can meet the needs of rural telecom carriers for quick and easy rollout. Because of its unique features, RuralStar has been widely adopted, making it possible for people in remote areas to connect with the

Huawei workers installing a RuralStar base station in a remote village in Guinea

---

① This is an excerpt from *Sustainability Report 2020* published by Huawei, which aims to promote its commitment to sustainability efforts, thus associating its brand image with ethical corporate conducts.

outside world.

For example, in Ghana, the lives of people in one village have been transformed since we built a RuralStar base station there. The base station was put up in just three days, and cost 70% less than a conventional cell tower. In Nigeria, people in Tobolo have been enjoying a better quality of life because RuralStar allows them to communicate with the outside world and brings them business opportunities.

In Thailand, RuralStar allows children in mountainous areas to watch videos on mobile phones and reach out to the outside world. In China, RuralStar has made it possible for residents in the Daliang Mountains to chat online, and for workers on the remote Zhoushan Islands to keep in touch with their families. RuralStar delivers connectivity to wide plains, steep hills, inhospitable deserts, remote islands, isolated rural areas, warren-like old towns, long highways, and deep tunnels, allowing people there to benefit from the digital world.

In 2020, Huawei launched the innovative RuralStar Pro solution, which helps bring high-quality mobile broadband services to remote villages. The solution's innovative integrated access and backhaul design reduces power consumption per site to 100 watts, greatly reducing end-to-end costs.

RuralStar Pro is already in use in customer projects, and is making a huge difference in the digital development of rural areas. To date, our RuralStar series solutions have provided mobile Internet services to more than 50 million people living in remote areas in over 60 countries and regions. (556 words)

Writing: Select one company that you are familiar with, and write a brief report on its ethical marketing activities. As for the format of the report, you can refer to the above excerpt of Huawei's sustainability report.

Word limit: 300 words.

Unit 5

Marketing Environment

🔔 Quote of the Unit:

"Many companies have forgotten they sell to actual people. Humans care about the entire experience, not just the marketing or sales or service. To really win in the modern age, you must solve for humans."

—Dharmesh Shah, CTO & co-founder, HubSpots

🔔 Learning Objectives:

1. Understand major factors of marketing environment, as well as the categorization of them.
2. Understand the major instrument (PEST) for marketing environment analysis.
3. Apply both the knowledge and language learned to analyze marketing environment cases and express your ideas properly and appropriately.

🔔 Pre-class Questions:

1. If one company plans to introduce its products to a new market, say, a foreign market, then what factors do the marketers need to know about this new market?
2. Among these factors, what factors should the marketers pay more attention to? Have you got any examples to illustrate them?

Text A: Lead-in

Learning Resources

Chinese Electric Vehicle Makers Aiming to Fill Europe's Supply Shortfall

By Ryan Thompson

When shopping for a new car, German drivers rarely **stray** from domestic brands. However, a booming interest in greener, all-electric engines could threaten the market **dominance** of the country's largest auto makers.

Volkswagen, Mercedes and Opel cars have been among the best-selling vehicles in Germany for decades. More than 55 percent of cars on the road were made domestically in 2020, according to registration information.

However, fewer than 15 of the nearly 100 different models built and designed in Germany are available with an electric engine. Electric vehicles are expected to account for 19 percent of all cars in Europe by 2025 and many auto makers in other parts of the **bloc** are modernizing their **fleets** to fall in line with new EU emissions rules that will take effect that year.

"German auto makers are obliged to meet a certain level of average CO_2 emissions and they're prepared to meet this minimum level and not necessarily go above that," said Matthias Schmidt, a European automotive market analyst. "This means that they're not prepared to bring a huge amount of electric vehicle supply to market because **internal combustion engines** at the moment are more profitable."

The focus on profit in the short term is leaving a gap for new brands to try their hand with electric vehicle (EV) car buyers in Europe. Aiways is one of multiple Chinese start-ups that embraced European design and paired it with Chinese-made EV technology.

"We started this vehicle with Europe in mind already," said Alexander Klose, Aiways' vice president for overseas. "It was always planned for the Chinese to go to the European market so it had to be engineered and designed for European **specifications**. We have a lot of European partners and European suppliers."

The Aiways fleet consists of a single model, the electric U5 SUV, which retails for $46,000. Additional models are planned for launch in 2022 and 2023.

Aiways is not alone in trying to bring Chinese technology to European roads. A growing number of Chinese EV manufacturers such as NIO and BYD are hoping to **capture** a piece of the European market. Both brands have announced they will begin sales in Norway, where EV ownership has led the way in the **European Single Market**, from September.

NIO has been called China's leading challenger to Tesla. Its IPO on US markets proved popular. Meanwhile, BYD is backed by billionaire investor Warren Buffet. Both brands say they intend to compete on quality as much as price.

Despite those efforts, auto analysts warn that all three Chinese car makers may be competing for the same type of customer in Europe and a crowded field of Chinese-made cars may hurt efforts to capture the market.

"It's going to be a case of differentiating themselves and not being cast in the same Chinese bubble as their competitors," said Schmidt.

There are also questions about whether European customers are ready for their cars to be 100 percent "Made in China".

Previous attempts to sell Chinese designed and made vehicles in Europe have failed miserably. Great Wall tried to market its SUVs in Italy but sold only a few hundred a year.

Aiways executives say they are confident their brand will not face the same issues.

"There already was a first attempt of Chinese cars to enter the European market and it was just not quite the time yet. I think within these 10 to 15 years a lot happened," said Kemal Yegenoglu, Aiways marketing director.

"If you look at these cars now, we're basically being tested by very renowned car magazines in Germany and we see how positively they rank us when it comes to **craftsmanship**, **build**, quality, safety," he added.　　(626 words)

(**Source:** https://newseu.cgtn.com/news/2021-10-21/Chinese-electric-vehicle-makers-aiming-to-fill-Europe-demand-shortfall-13gHp1cPOrC/index.html.)

Vocabulary and Useful Expressions

stray /streɪ/	*v.*	if your mind or your eyes stray, you do not concentrate on or look at one particular subject, but start thinking about or looking at other things　走神，（视线）偏离，往别处看

dominance /ˈdɒmɪnəns/	*n.*	the dominance of a particular person or thing is the fact that they are more powerful, successful, or important than other people or things 支配，控制
bloc /blɒk/	*n.*	a group of countries that work closely together because they have similar political interests （政治利益一致的）国家集团
fleet /fliːt/	*n.*	a fleet of vehicles is a group of them, especially when they all belong to a particular organization or business, or when they are all going somewhere together 车队
internal combustion engine		an internal combustion engine is an engine that creates its energy by burning fuel inside itself 内燃机
specification /ˌspesɪfɪˈkeɪʃn/	*n.*	a detailed description of how sth. is, or should be, designed or made 规格，规范，明细单，说明书
capture /ˈkæptʃə(r)/	*v.*	if you capture something that you are trying to obtain in competition with other people, you succeed in obtaining it 夺得，获得，得到
European Single Market		The European Single Market, Internal Market or Common Market is a single market comprising the 27 member states of the European Union (EU) as well as—with certain exceptions—Iceland, Liechtenstein, and Norway through the Agreement on the European Economic Area, and Switzerland through bilateral treaties. The single market seeks to guarantee the free movement of goods, capital, services, and people, known collectively as the "four freedom". 欧洲单一市场
craftsmanship /ˈkrɑːftsmənʃɪp/	*n.*	craftsmanship is the quality that something has when it is beautiful and has been very carefully made 精工细作
build /bɪld/	*n.*	someone's build is the shape that their bones and muscles give to their body 体形，体格，身材（本文采用其比喻义）

Exercise 1. Knowledge: Answer the following questions briefly according to the above article.

Read the article carefully and write down the information below after each category of the marketing environment for Chinese EV manufacturers when they attempt to enter the European market.

1. Competitor's performance:

2. Environmental concern:

3. Consumers:

4. Legal conditions:

5. Trade treaty:

6. Partners and suppliers:

7. What leaves a market gap:

Exercise 2. Language: Fill in the blanks with words or expressions from the above article.

1. A market _____ is a chance to create and offer something currently unavailable.
2. The two maverick tourists _____ away from the tour group to look at some ancient sculptures.
3. The emergence of startup EV manufacturers has already threatened the market _____ of traditional car manufacturing giants.
4. I really appreciate the skills of engineering and _____ of the new car.

5. Some Chinese EV manufacturers planning to go to the European market need to engineer and design their cars for European _____.
6. More models EV are planned for _____ in 2022 and 2023.
7. More than 30 of the nearly 100 different models built and designed in China are _____ with an electric engine.
8. The new product should fall in line with new EU environmental rules that will take _____ next year.
9. Car manufacturers are obliged to meet a certain level of average CO_2 _____ if they want to continue to sell their cars in EU.
10. Chinese EV makers identify a market _____ in the EU car market where traditional car makers are not willing to make and sell more EV cars since cars with internal combustion engines are more profitable.

Text B: Intensive Reading

Marketing Environment: Explanation, Components, & Importance

"A company's marketing environment consists of the actors and forces outside of marketing that affect marketing management ability to build and maintain successful relationships with target customers."

— Philip Kotler

What Is Marketing Environment?

In brief, marketing environment is the combination of both external and internal factors and forces that affect one company's ability to create and deliver values to customers and remain competitive and profitable.

The marketing environment consists of both internal and external environments. The internal environment is company-specific and includes owners, workers, machines, materials, etc. The external environment is further divided into two levels, micro-environment and macro-environment, according to whether they can affect one business directly.

The micro-environment is also company-specific but external to the business. It consists of factors engaged in manufacturing, distributing and promoting the product.

The macro-environment includes larger societal forces and factors such as **demographic**, economic, physical, technological, political-legal and **sociocultural** environment.

Internal Environment

The internal environment of the business includes all the forces and factors inside the company which affect its marketing operations directly. These components can be labeled as the 5 Ms:

Men: Human resource of the company, including staff from all functional departments.
Minutes: Time taken for the processes of the business to complete.
Machinery: Equipment required to facilitate or complete the processes.
Materials: Supplies required by the business to complete the business processes.
Money: Financial resources used to purchase machinery, materials, and pay the employees.

External Environment

The external environment consists of factors and forces which are external to the business and beyond the control of it. The external environment is of two types: micro-environment and macro-environment.

Micro-environment

The micro-component of the external environment is also known as the task environment. It consists of external forces and factors that are directly related to the business. These include stakeholders such as suppliers, market **intermediaries**, customers, partners, competitors and the public.

Suppliers include all the parties which provide resources needed by the company.

Market intermediaries include parties involved in distributing the product or service of the company.

Partners are all the separate entities like advertising agencies, market research agencies, banking and insurance companies, transportation companies, brokers, etc.

Customers are the target group of the company. The aim of the entire value delivery system is to serve target customers and create strong relationships with them.

Competitors are the players in the same market who target similar segments of customers.

Marketers must do more than simply adapt to the needs of target consumers. They also must gain strategic advantage by positioning their offers strongly against competitors' offerings in the minds of customers.

A public is any group that has an actual or potential interest in or impact on the organization's ability to achieve its objectives. For example, financial **publics**, government publics, local publics, citizen's action groups.

Macro-environment

The macro-environment consists of external factors and forces which affect the industry as a whole but don't have a direct impact on the business. The macro-environment can be divided into 6 parts.

Demographic Environment

Demographic environment refers to the human population characteristics that surround a firm or nation and greatly affect markets. The demographic environment includes such factors as age distributions, births, deaths, immigration, marital status, gender, education, religious affiliations and geographic dispersion — characteristics often used for segmentation purposes.

Economic Environment

The economic environment consists of factors that influence customers' purchasing power and spending patterns. These factors include the GDP, CPI, interest rates, foreign exchange rates, **inflation**, income distribution, government funding and **subsidies**, and other major economic variables. In addition, bigger economic considerations include business cycles, **recessions**, and both national and global **fiscal** policies.

Natural Environment

Natural environment refers to natural resources that are needed as inputs by marketers or that are affected by marketing activities. This includes the accessibility to natural resources, climatic conditions, environmental change, natural disasters, pollution, restrictions on carbon-dioxide emission, etc.

Technological Environment

The technological environment consists of innovation, research and development in technology, technological alternatives, innovation **inducements** and technological barriers to smooth operation. Technology is one of the biggest sources of opportunities and threats for the company. Given the current situation, in which technological environment is changing very rapidly, once a company is lagged behind, the chances might be it would lose the competition.

Political Environment

The political environment includes laws and government policies prevailing in the country. It also includes other pressure groups and agencies which influence or limit the working of the industry and/or the business in the society. An example is the various codes and regulations imposed on different industrial sectors. A typical example is the construction industrial sector where obligatory administrative rules specify the means of operations.

Sociocultural Environment

The sociocultural aspect of the macro-environment is made up of culture, attitudes, lifestyles, interests, religion, prejudice, perceived values and beliefs of different people. For instance, in western cultures that encourage people to maintain a lean physique, the market for diet products, fitness equipment and fitness services may boom. On the other hand, such a market might not experience much success in a place where the people are not as passionate about losing weight. This differs from region to region, people to people and culture to culture.

Importance of Marketing Environment

Every business, no matter how big or small, operates within the marketing environment. Its present and future existence, profits, image, and positioning depend on its internal and external environment. The business environment is one of the most dynamic aspects of the business. In order to operate and stay in the market for long, one has to understand and analyze the marketing environment and its components properly.   (935 words)

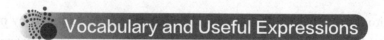

demographic /ˌdeməˈgræfɪk/	*a.*	of or relating to a statistic characterizing human populations (or segments of human populations broken down by age, sex, income, etc.) 人口统计（学）的
sociocultural /ˌsəʊsɪəʊˈkʌltʃərəl/	*a.*	relating to both social and cultural matters 社会文化的

Unit 5 Marketing Environment

intermediary	/ˌɪntəˈmiːdɪərɪ/	*n.*	(between A and B) a person or an organization that helps other people or organizations to make an agreement by being a means of communication between them 中间人，调解人
publics	/ˈpʌblɪks/	*n.*	Publics are small groups of people who follow one or more particular issue very closely. 公众，……界
inflation	/ɪnˈfleɪʃn/	*n.*	a general rise in the prices of services and goods in a particular country, resulting in a fall in the value of money; the rate at which this happens 通货膨胀，通胀率
subsidy	/ˈsʌbsədɪ/	*n.*	money that is paid by a government or an organization to reduce the costs of services or of producing goods so that their prices can be kept low 补贴，补助金，津贴
fiscal	/ˈfɪskl/	*a.*	connected with government or public money, especially taxes 财政的，国库的
recession	/rɪˈseʃn/	*n.*	a difficult time for the economy of a country, when there is less trade and industrial activity than usual and more people are unemployed 经济衰退，经济萎缩
inducement	/ɪnˈdjuːsmənt/	*n.*	something that is given to sb. to persuade them to do sth. (~ to sb.; ~ to do sth.) 引诱，刺激，诱因

Exercise 1. Language: Find out the synonyms for the following words.

1. inducement: _____
2. inflation: _____
3. recession: _____
4. subsidy: _____
5. fiscal: _____
6. intermediary: _____
7. stakeholder: _____
8. obligatory: _____
9. accessibility: _____
10. affiliation: _____

Exercise 2. Knowledge: Translate the following sentences into Chinese.

1. The external environment is further divided into two levels, micro-environment and macro-environment, according to whether they can affect one business directly.

2. The macro-environment includes larger societal forces and factors such as demographic, economic, physical, technological, political-legal and sociocultural environment.

3. The internal environment of the business includes all the forces and factors inside the company which affect its marketing operations directly.

4. These factors include the GDP, CPI, interest rates, foreign exchange rates, inflation, income distribution, government funding and subsidies, and other major economic variables.

5. The technological environment consists of innovation, research and development in technology, technological alternatives, innovation inducements and technological barriers to smooth operation.

Oral practice: Work with your partners. After reading the above article, you may have already understood the importance of analyzing marketing environment factors. Imagine that you work for a company, and discuss how the micro-environmental players may affect a company's business. You can suggest a possible scenario and explain your ideas. You are encouraged to use both the language and knowledge learned in this unit.

Unit 5 Marketing Environment

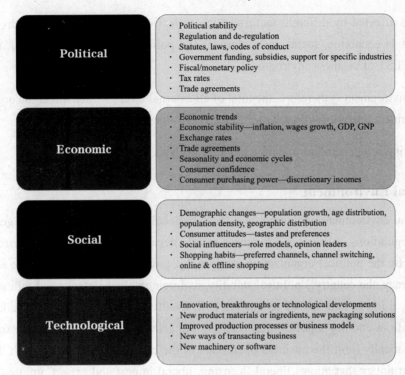

Text C: Extensive Reading

Learning Resources

The PEST Analysis of Burberry

Company Background

Burberry is a British luxury fashion house headquartered in London, England. was founded in 1856 by Thomas Burberry in Basingstoke, Hampshire, England. By 1870, the business had established itself by focusing on the development of outdoor attire.

It currently designs and distributes ready-to-wear products, including trench coats, leather goods, footwear, fashion accessories, eyewear, fragrances, and cosmetics across the world. Burberry has more than 500 stores in more than 20 countries. Being listed on the London Stock Exchange, Burberry is a component of the FTSE 100 Index. It has utilized licensing and brand extensions to appeal to younger customers.

Analysis

Business is affected by different factors which collectively form the business environment. These include economic, social, technological and political factors. Put together, marketers call it the PEST of business environment.

Business environment is therefore, the total of all external forces, which affect the organization and the business operations directly or indirectly (Kotler & Armstrong, 2004).

The following is a general introduction to PEST analysis.

1. Political Environment

The political environment, including laws (both national and international ones), government policies, regulations, influences a business to a larger extent. This political environment is influenced by the political organization, philosophy, government ideology, nature and extent of bureaucracy, the country's political stability, its foreign policy, defense and military policy, the country's image and that of its leaders both locally and internationally (Shaikh, 2010). For example, a country's policy that restricts the growth of multinationals in the market will automatically limit the business operations of the company hence its growth. Similarly, government policy that allows liberal licensing, liberal import and export, inflow of foreign capital and technology, can actually encourage the expansion of business operation in that country. Burberry was able to establish its first foreign outlets in Paris, the United States and South America, and export its first shipment of raincoat to Japan as well as China just because of the globalization policies adopted by the governments of these countries.

Legal factors involve how flexible and adaptable the law and legal rules that govern the business are. Legal provisions may also contribute to one company's income depending on the environment of operation. For example, Burberry makes a considerable portion of its income from licensing, which is made possible because of laws and regulations allowing it to charge licensing fee legally in its foreign destinations of operation.

2. Economic Environment

Economic factors include the country's economic system, its structures, and economic policies, how the capital market is organized, and nature of factors of production, business cycles, and very importantly, its socioeconomic infrastructure. Any successful organization pictures out the external factors that affect the business, anticipates the prospective market situations and works hard to minimize the costs while maximizing the profits. When Burberry noticed the high demand of rainwear, it utilized this opportunity increasing its production in the market.

Changes in demand are also one great factor that determines business performance. It is undeniable that all business and non-business organizations felt the impact of the 2008 global financial tsunami. Burberry experienced a trough just like any other business during that period.

3. Social Environment

Sociological factors establish the culture of work, labor mobility, work groups, etc., hence, business operation of an enterprise. These factors include cost structure, customs and conventions, cultural heritage, peoples' view towards wealth and income and scientific methods, seniority respect, mobility of labor (Shaikh, 2010). All these factors have big impact on business. For example, peoples' demand, which determines what kind of products to be offered, is affected by peoples' attitudes, customs, cultural values, fashion and other related forces. The code of conduct that is supposed to be followed by the business is also determined by the sociocultural environment.

The social changes in life also lead to new fashion trends that affect business in any part of the economy. Burberry has grasped the opportunity of changing attitudes towards fashion and luxury due to rapid growth of wealth in emerging markets, hence increased its business scope, which resulted in greater profitability.

4. Technological Environment

Technological factors, including technological investment, technological application and the effect of technology on markets, can greatly affect the development of business. The type and quality of goods to be produced and the type and quality of plant and equipment to be used in a company, is determined by the kind of technology employed by that company (Mühlbacher, Dahringer & Leihs, 2006). Burberry keeps extending its web reach so that its customers worldwide can view its brands. For example, the company is targeting the Chinese shoppers directly by launching a website in China. This is because this target market accounts for 30% of sales in its London stores (Burberry, 2012).   (785 words)

(**Source:** Burberry. Burberry Ltd.[EB/OL] (2012-06-06) [2022-06-19]. http://www.funduniverse.com/company-histories/burberry-ltd-company-history.html; KOTLER P, ARMSTRONG G. Principles of marketing[M]. Upper Saddle River, New Jersey: Prentice Hall, 2004; SHAIKH S. Business environment[M]. New Delhi: Pearson, 2010; https://www.paypervids.com/factors-influence-business-environment/.)

Writing: A US-based multinational sportswear company intends to expand its business in China, considering that China is already the biggest market for sports products. The country has the largest sports population in the world. In order to help decision makers in the headquarters know more about the marketing environment of China, you are hired to conduct a STEP analysis on it. Please write briefly about the STEP factors of China. As for format, you can refer to the text above.

Word limit: 500 words.

Unit 6

Legal Aspects of Marketing

🔔 Quote of the Unit:

"The end of law is not to abolish or restrain, but to preserve and enlarge freedom."

—John Locke

🔔 Learning Objectives:

1. Understand the concept of intellectual property right and its importance.
2. Understand major types of IPR, as well as the names of crimes related to the violation of these rights respectively.
3. Use both the knowledge and language learned in this unit to discuss IPR issues in marketing.

🔔 Pre-class Questions:

1. Have you ever bought any fake products without knowing? If yes, how did you feel when you found out the truth?
2. Have you ever bought any books not legally printed? If yes, how did you feel when you found out the truth?
3. Do you know making and selling fake products is a crime? If yes, do you know the name of the crime?
4. Do you know printing a book and selling it in the market without the author's permission is a crime? If yes, do you know the name of the crime?

Unit 6 Legal Aspects of Marketing

Text A: Lead-in

Cases of Fake Products

Learning Resources

Millions of dollars are spent every year by companies fighting the sale of fake products.

From fake Gucci® and Louis Vuitton® bags on street corners to **name-brand** cosmetics sold at **flea markets**, fake goods can be found almost everywhere — including huge online trading and retailing platforms such as eBay and Amazon.

Many of these players continue to confront problems of fake products. Below are some cases collected from news reports.

1. Amazon Takes Fake Product Sellers to Court for the First Time

If you didn't know that Amazon was having a problem of fake products, then 2016 was the year to find out. The largest Internet-based retailer in the world was considered a reliably safe source of goods, but more growing concern of this problem forced the company to take legal action.

The e-commerce giant **filed a lawsuit** against fake product sellers after a growing chorus of **genuine** product sellers was concerned that **knockoffs** were hurting their sales by **deterring** customers. A patented product and athletic training supplies were a few of the products in question in the suit.

Though the case will surely not put an end to its problem with fake products, the suit should at least deter some **fraudsters** from making profits from the IP of others.

2. A $70 Million Fake Currency Ring Gets Busted

When we think of products, we tend to think of goods, wares and services. But one of the biggest fake problems in the world lies in fake currency, or fake money.

Reported this year was the downfall of the best-known team of **forgers** for U.S. currency, whose fake money is still in circulation today.

Fake money had something of a "Golden Age" around the time of the Civil War, when banks issued their own currency. Back then, 1 in 3 bills in circulation was fake.

Today's best fake currencies have an amazing attention to detail. Though fake money is far more tempered than it used to be, as the case in China where people use digital currency instead of paper ones, it's still so vital to fight the problem in other countries and maintain the integrity of currency.

3. Fashion Designer Wins $90 Million in **Damages** after Successfully Suing Nearly 50 Defendants

In a trademark dispute and **cybersquatting** case, Alexander Wang — a high-profile designer — won $90 million from nearly 50 owners of 459 sites selling knockoffs of his handbags, footwear, apparel and accessories.

Since 2005, Wang put his time, talent and money into creating a distinctive brand that fake product makers wanted to profit from. This case clearly shows how expensive it can be to profit from knockoff goods, and how peddlers have to think twice when selling fake Wang products. (454 words)

Vocabulary and Useful Expressions

name-brand /neɪm brænd/	a.	relating to or being a product that is made by a well-known company 名牌的
flea market		an outdoor market that sells second-hand (= old or used) goods at low prices 跳蚤市场（廉价出售旧物的露天市场）
file a lawsuit		to start a process by which a court of law makes a decision to end a disagreement between people or organizations 提起诉讼，打官司
genuine /ˈdʒenjuɪn/	a.	real; exactly what it appears to be; not artificial 真的，名副其实的
knockoff /ˈnɒkɔːf/	n.	a cheap copy of a well-known product （廉价）冒牌货，仿制品
deter /dɪˈtɜː(r)/	v.	to make sb. decide not to do sth. or continue doing sth., especially by making them understand the difficulties and unpleasant results of their actions 制止，阻止，威慑，使不敢
fraudster /ˈfrɔːdstə(r)/	n.	a person who commits fraud 犯欺诈罪者，犯欺骗罪者
forger /ˈfɔːdʒə(r)/	n.	a person who makes illegal copies of money, documents, etc. in order to cheat people 伪造者，犯伪造罪的人

Unit 6 Legal Aspects of Marketing

damages /ˈdæmɪdʒɪz/	n.	(pl) an amount of money that a court decides should be paid to sb. by the person, company, etc. that has caused them harm or injury （法院判定的）损害赔偿金
cybersquatting /ˈsaɪbəskwɒtɪŋ/	n.	the buying of an Internet domain name that might be wanted by another person, business, or organization with the intention of selling it to them and making a profit 抢注网络域名

Exercise 1. Language: Fill in the blanks with words or expressions from the above article.

1. The company decided to file a _____ against the manufacturers that made fake products wearing the company's brand name.
2. He was ruled not guilty in court and _____ of $1 million were awarded.
3. The machine works steady because _____ electric parts are employed.
4. This notorious _____ convinced people to invest millions in his scheme.
5. They attended the _____ market yesterday and finally sold the used sofa.
6. If you visit those peddlers, you may have the chance to buy a _____ watch from them.
7. _____ means malicious intent or the improper registration or use of a distinctive trademark or other Internet domain name.
8. The passage of this new law is expected to _____ gun-related crime.
9. After years of efforts, the _____ of currency is finally arrested by the police.
10. Though theft and robbery are more _____ in China these days, it is still necessary to remind citizens of the potential crimes.

Exercise 2. Knowledge: Answer the following questions briefly according to the above article.

1. How serious is the problem of fake products?
   _____
   _____

2. How did major retailing platforms combat this phenomenon?
   _____
   _____

3. What was the response of genuine product sellers against fake product selling?

4. What problem did Alexander Wang encounter? What does this case reflect?

5. What happened to the problem of making and using fake money in China? What is the major cause?

Text B: Intensive Reading

Legal Aspects of Marketing

Learning Resources

When you read the word "legal", you may realize that this word is related to law. Yes, it is true. Not only the word "legal", some other words like "**legality**", "**legitimate**", "**legislation**" are all related to law.

Being legal means being lawful, being in harmony with law. Law is a system of rules that are enforced through social institutions such as police system, **judicial** system, and jails. Law is there to govern and regulate behaviors. When it comes to marketing, laws are also applicable.

Today's market is highly competitive with many companies providing similar products to similar or overlapping target customers. Therefore, marketers may try to seek for and use the latest aggressive marketing tactics, resulting in a kind of competition that is not fair. To go ahead, **ambush** marketing or **deceptive** advertising are often in unauthorized use with the aim of putting other organizations in disadvantages. This is also a reason why many governments across the globe made special laws to avoid unfair trade practices and to regulate anti-competitive business practices.

In order to protect an invention, idea, **ingenuity** or a creative product against unfair trade practices, copyrights, trademarks and patents were engaged as a law of **intellectual property**. Altogether people call them the intellectual property right. They give exclusive rights to own and make use of the creations of the mind (such as symbols, designs, drawings, paintings, pictures, writings and so on) and discoveries a person has made.

These rights grant the protection of the product of one's intellect. According to the World Intellectual Property Organization, intellectual property refers to creations of the mind: inventions, literary and artistic works, and symbols, names, images and designs used in commerce.

Please pay attention to the words "in commerce", this means only when the ideas are used to make money the concept of intellectual property will apply. Intellectual property can be divided into two categories, namely industrial property and copyright.

Industrial property includes **patents** and **trademarks**.

Patent gives the exclusive right to make, use and sell an invention in a given geographical area. A granted patent gives patent protection for a certain period of time.

The patent holder needs to **renew** the patent upon its **expiry**; otherwise, the patent will be open to anyone who wants to use.

A trademark can include words and/or symbols that help differentiate a company's product from others'. A registered trademark is one that has been recognized and protected by the authorities.

Copyright protects literary and artistic works, including novels, plays, films, musical works, artistic works such as drawings, photographs, and architectural designs.

If one work is protected by copyright, we can either say this work is subject to copyright, or this work is copyrighted. Legal problems may arise if someone (or a legal person) uses copyright protected work or patent of another person or company without owner's permission. Using one's intellectual property without asking for permission is an infringement upon intellectual property right.

Intellectual property crimes include **counterfeiting** and **piracy**. Counterfeiting is **deliberate** or wilful infringement upon trademark. If someone counterfeits something, they make a version of it that is not genuine, but has been made to look genuine in order to deceive consumers. In other words, the producer of the counterfeited goods uses other famous trademarks to sell its own products with higher price. For example, some handbag producers may use famous trademarks like Gucci, LV to sell their counterfeited products, just aiming to earn extremely high profits.

Piracy is deliberate or wilful infringement upon copyright. It happens when one company reproduces copyrighted works without permission from the IP owner. For example, some publishers may provide best selling novels without having the permission from neither the author, nor the IP owning publisher. If the trademark or copyright holder believes that another person or company has made unauthorized use of trademark or copyrighted work then this may lead to a lawsuit.

Under such circumstances, the **infringed** may take the infringer to court to enforce the trademark or copyright. If the court of law rules the infringer is guilty he may have to pay damages or compensation to the infringed often in financial forms. In other words, the infringer needs to pay a sum for money to the infringed in order to make up for his losses caused by the infringer's illegal acts.

From the part of the consumers what if the consumers buy some products that are **defective** and not able to live up to the advertised standards? In some countries there are consumer protection laws to protect the interest of the consumers. For instance, in China, we have *Law of the People's Republic of China on the Protection of Consumers' Rights and Interests*; in the UK there is a *Consumer Protection Act*. Both of them protect the consumers from faulty or defective products or products that are not as safe as they are generally expected to be.

In this sense, consumers are legally **entitled** to goods of satisfactory quality. Producers, suppliers and importers are responsible for or legally liable for the products they sell.

Under such a law, if people are injured or physically hurt by a defective product then they do not need to prove a manufacturer negligent before suing. This is called the product **liability**, which is the central part of the law.

To sum up, this article mainly introduces the legal aspects of marketing especially the intellectual property right or IPR in short. IPR includes two categories namely the industrial property, including patent, trademark, and the copyright.

Any infringement upon either one of these rights will lead to lawsuits because governments across the globe formulate laws to protect intellectual property right and to encourage people to develop original ideas to improve our lives. Infringers of these rights, once convicted, should pay damages or compensation to the infringed parties. (972 words)

Vocabulary and Useful Expressions

legality /liːˈɡæləti/	*n.*	the fact of being legal （不可数名词）合法（性）
		the legal aspect of an action or a situation （可数名词，常用复数）（某行为或情况的）法律方面

legitimate /lɪˈdʒɪtɪmət/	a.	allowed and acceptable according to the law 合法的，法律认可的，法定的	
legislation /ˌledʒɪsˈleɪʃn/	n.	the process of making and passing laws 立法，制定法律	
judicial /dʒuˈdɪʃl/	a.	connected with a court, a judge or legal judgement 法庭的，法官的，审判的，司法的	
ambush /ˈæmbʊʃ/	n.	the act of hiding and waiting for sb. and then making a surprise attack on them 伏击，埋伏	
deceptive /dɪˈseptɪv/	a.	likely to make you believe sth. that is not true 欺骗性的，误导的，骗人的	
ingenuity /ˌɪndʒɪˈnjuːətɪ/	n.	the ability to invent things or solve problems in clever new ways 独创力，聪明才智，心灵手巧	
intellectual property		(law) an idea, a design, etc. that sb. has created and that the law prevents other people from copying （法律）知识财产	
patent /ˈpeɪtnt; ˈpætnt/	n.	an official right to be the only person to make, use or sell a product or an invention; a document that proves this 专利权，专利证书	
trademark /ˈtreɪdmɑːk/	n.	a name, symbol or design that a company uses for its products and that cannot be used by anyone else 商标	
renew /rɪˈnjuː/	v.	to make sth. valid for a further period of time 使继续有效，延长……的期限	
expiry /ɪkˈspaɪərɪ/	n.	an ending of the period of time when an official document can be used, or when an agreement is valid （文件、协议等的）满期，届期，到期	
copyright /ˈkɒpɪraɪt/	n.	if a person or an organization holds the copyright on a piece of writing, music, etc., they are the only people who have the legal right to publish, broadcast, perform it, etc., and other people must ask their permission to use it or any part of it 版权，著作权	
counterfeit /ˈkaʊntəfɪt/	v.	to make an exact copy of sth. in order to trick people into thinking that it is the real thing 伪造，仿造，制假	
piracy /ˈpaɪrəsɪ/	n.	the act of making illegal copies of video tapes, computer programs, books, etc., in order to sell them 盗版行为，非法复制	
deliberate /dɪˈlɪbərət/	a.	done on purpose rather than by accident 故意的，蓄意的，存心的	

infringe /ɪnˈfrɪndʒ/	v.	to limit sb.'s legal rights (~ on/upon sth.) 侵犯，侵害（合法权益）
defective /dɪˈfektɪv/	a.	having a fault or faults; not perfect or complete 有缺点的，有缺陷的，有毛病的
entitle /ɪnˈtaɪtl/	v.	to give sb. the right to have or to do sth. (~ sb. to sth.) 使享有权利，使符合资格
liability /ˌlaɪəˈbɪlətɪ/	n.	the state of being legally responsible for sth. (~ for sth.; ~ to do sth.) （法律上对某事物的）责任，义务

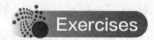

Exercises

Exercise 1. Language: List some words that share some common word roots with the following words as many as you can. One example is already done for your reference. You can refer to the dictionary or consult your partners for more resources.

Example:

Legal: legally, legality, legalize...

1. legislate: _____
2. legitimate: _____
3. law: _____
4. judicial: _____
5. deceptive: _____
6. authority: _____
7. intellectual: _____
8. infringe: _____
9. defect: _____
10. register: _____

Exercise 2. Language: The following sentence can be expressed in three different ways. Write down the other two sentences. You can refer to the above article for more information.

This novel is protected by copyright.

1. _____
2. _____

Exercise 3. Knowledge: True or false statements. If the following statements are true, write T; if false, write F.

1. Once a company register for patent successfully, it is granted with patent protection across the globe. ( )
2. Copyright is granted to the creations of the mind including artistic works, literary works, paintings, photographs, illustrations, musical compositions, sound recordings, computer programs, books, poems, blog posts, movies, architectural works, and plays. ( )
3. After the expiry date one needs to renew the patent, which means to apply for a new patent. ( )
4. Piracy is deliberate or wilful infringement upon trademark. ( )
5. Product liability allows consumers to sue manufacturers for the harm caused by using their defective products, without the need to prove the latter's negligence. ( )
6. In a lawsuit concerning IPR, the infringed may be ruled to pay compensation to the infringer. ( )
7. Counterfeiting is deliberate or wilful infringement upon patent. ( )
8. Unauthorized use of trademark or copyrighted work may lead to a lawsuit. ( )
9. The producer of the counterfeited goods uses other famous trademarks to sell its own products with higher price. ( )
10. A registered trademark is one that has been recognized and protected by the authorities. ( )

Exercise 4. Knowledge: Fill in the blanks with words or expressions from the above article.

1. The ability to manage the market effectively and smoothly is the most important factor for a company to decide whether or not to _____ the contract.
2. I just wonder whether this leather belt is made of _____ leather or not.
3. When a writer publishes a novel, he is automatically granted the _____ of the book.
4. A manufacturer negligently assembled and marketed a car with _____ window shield which may break easily.
5. The law firm, which specializes in IPR cases, can help the company handle patent and trademark _____.
6. Product _____ is the legal responsibility imposed on a business for the manufacturing or selling of defective goods.
7. _____ is a criminal offense that involves fraudulently manufacturing and distributing an item of lesser value than the genuine product, usually for the purpose of monetary gain.
8. _____ is the act of illegally reproducing or disseminating copyrighted

material, such as computer programs, books, music, and films.
9. A _____ act of infringement upon one's copyright will lead to a lawsuit.
10. _____ marketing is the use of false and/or misleading information to capture the attention of the consumer through the usage of false information to persuade buyers into a business transaction.

Oral practice: Work with your partners, and take turns to share your knowledge or experience of IPR infringement cases—be it piracy or counterfeiting. You can search online for resources, including texts, pictures or diagrams. Discuss with your partners, what harms these IPR infringements may do to IP owners.

Text C: Extensive Reading

Learning Resources

Top 5 Intellectual Property Disputes

By Heleigh Bostwick

Intellectual property is becoming more and more valuable and protecting intellectual property rights is becoming more important — and more difficult — as time goes by. The rise of the Internet is a major force behind the increase in intellectual property disputes.

Let's have a look at the top 5 intellectual property disputes both on and off the Internet.

1. Amazon's 1-click Patent

Amazon was granted a patent for 1-click technology on September 28, 1999. Also known as one-click buying, the technology allows customers to make an online purchase in a single click — without having to manually input billing and shipping information every time they purchase a product. Instead, 1-click uses a billing address and credit card or other payment info that is kept on file in the user's account.

There have been several patent disputes surrounding 1-click technology, including a patent infringement lawsuit filed against Barnes & Noble in 1999 — only a month after Amazon's patent was issued. Barnes & Noble offered a checkout option called "Express Lane", which also enabled shoppers to make a purchase with one click. The lawsuit was settled in 2002; however, the terms were not disclosed.

2. Google Trademark Keywords

In April 2009, the 2nd U.S. Circuit Court of Appeals issued a ruling stating that Google must continue in a trademark infringement lawsuit brought on by Rescuecom. In the lawsuit, Google is accused of selling the trademarked name "Rescuecom" as a keyword to Rescuecom's competitors. The keywords are used to deliver Google's sponsored search results, therefore allowing competitors to appear on the results page when a user searches for "Rescuecom". The lawsuit was originally filed in 2006 and dismissed by the lower courts.

This isn't the first time Google has found itself in the same legal predicament. Both American Airlines and Geico have sued Google over selling their trademarks as keywords. Google's trademark policy has gone through several iterations as the company attempts to find a balance that protects trademarks, yet allows retailers to advertise the trademarked goods they sell.

3. The *Da Vinci Code* Case

In the famous *Da Vinci Code* court case of Michael Baigent and Richard Leigh vs. the Random House Group Limited, Baigent and Leigh alleged that Dan Brown, author of the bestselling *Da Vinci Code*, infringed on the copyright of their non-fiction work, *Holy Blood, Holy Grail*. Because Brown had not copied the text of the earlier book, the claim was based on "non-literal" copying — Baigent and Leigh asserted that Brown told his story in the same "manner" in which they had expressed historical facts in their book.

The claimants' case was dismissed in 2006 with the judgment stating in part that "... there is no copyright infringement either by textual copying or non textual copying of a substantial part of HBHG..."

4. Napster

In one of the Internet's the most well-known intellectual property cases, the Recording Industry Association of America (RIAA) sued Napster, a file-sharing site. Founded in 1999, Napster allowed users to share music files and thousands of people began downloading songs for free rather than buying CDs.

However, Napster did not own the rights to the music that people were uploading to its servers, where the music was stored and ultimately shared. The rights were owned by the recording artists and recording studios. The RIAA sued Napster and won, causing Napster to close its doors — or its servers, as the case may be. Napster now operates as a fee-based music download site and pays licensing fees for the music it sells.

5. Bratz Dolls vs. Barbie

In 2008, Barbie was finally declared the winner in the long-running intellectual property rights battle between Mattel, Inc. and MGA Entertainment Inc., the makers of Barbie dolls and Bratz dolls, respectively. In the lawsuit, Mattel sued MGA claiming that MGA stole the concept and the name of the Bratz doll from them.

Carter Bryant, designer of the Bratz doll, was an employee of Mattel, but also working as a consultant for MGA when he designed the doll. A few years after MGA began selling Bratz, Mattel sued both Bryant and MGA alleging copyright infringement. Because Bryant was on the Mattel payroll when he created the doll, the Bratz name and design are considered trade secrets. The courts sided with Mattel and ordered MGA to pay $100 million in damages.   (722 words)

(**Source:** https://www.legalzoom.com/articles/top-5-intellectual-property-disputes.)

Writing: After reading the above cases, you may have already found out the complicated nature of IPR disputes, and related solutions to these problems. Please write a brief report on how should IP owners do to protect their IPR. You can refer to the article above, as well as other sources. You are encouraged to use both the language and knowledge learned in this unit.

Try to make your writing reasonable and logically connected.

Word limit: 500 words.

Unit 7

Marketing Research

🔔 *Quote of the Unit:*

"Marketing without data is like driving with your eyes closed."

—Dan Zarrella, social media scientist

🔔 *Learning Objectives:*

1. Understand key concepts and expressions associated with marketing research.
2. Understand different types of marketing research.
3. Conduct a mini marketing research by applying both the knowledge and language learned in this unit.

🔔 *Pre-class Questions:*

1. Have you ever been involved in one marketing research?
2. Do you know the purpose of conducting a marketing research?
3. What types of marketing research technique do you already know?
4. Do you know the difference between a marketing research and a market research?

Text A: Lead-in

Importance of Marketing Research

Learning Resources

Research, as a general concept, is the process of gathering information to learn about something that is not fully known yet. Nearly everyone **engages** in some sort of research. From the highly trained geologist investigating newly discovered earthquake faults, to the author of best-selling spy novels gaining insight into new **surveillance** techniques, to the model train **hobbyist** spending hours hunting down the manufacturer of an old electric engine, each is driven by the **quest** for information.

For marketers, research is not only used for the purpose of learning, it is also a critical **component** needed to make good decisions. Market research does this by giving marketers a picture of what is occurring (or likely to occur) and, when done well, offers **alternative** choices that can be made. For instance, good research may suggest multiple options for introducing new products or entering new markets. In most cases marketing decisions prove less risky (though they are never risk free) when the marketer can select from more than one option.

Using an **analogy** of a house foundation, marketing research can be viewed as the foundation of marketing decision making. Just as a well-built house requires a strong foundation to remain sturdy, marketing decisions need the support of research in order to be viewed favorably by customers and to stand up to competition and other external pressures. Consequently, all areas of marketing and all marketing decisions should be supported with some level of research.

While research is key to marketing decision making, it does not always need to be **elaborate** to be effective. Sometimes small efforts, such as doing a quick search on the Internet, will provide the needed information. However, for most marketers there are times when more elaborate research work is needed and understanding the right way to conduct research, whether performing the work themselves or hiring someone else to handle it (outsourcing), can increase the effectiveness of these projects.

Examples of Research in Marketing

As noted, marketing research is **undertaken** to support a wide variety of marketing decision making. The table below presents a small sampling of the research undertaken by marketers.

Marketing Decision	Types of Research
Target Markets	sales; market size; demand for product; customer characteristics; purchase behavior; customer satisfaction; website traffic
Product	product development; package protection; packaging awareness; brand name selection; brand recognition; brand preference; product positioning
Distribution	distributor interest; assessing shipping options; online shopping; retail store site selection
Promotion	advertising recall; advertising copy testing; sales promotion response rates; sales force compensation; traffic studies (outdoor advertising); public relations media placement
Pricing	price elasticity analysis; **optimal** price setting; discount options
External Factors	competitive analysis; legal environment; social and cultural trends
Other	company image; test marketing

(449 words)

Vocabulary and Useful Expressions

engage /ɪnˈgeɪdʒ/	v.	If you engage in an activity, you do it or are actively involved with it. 参加，参与
surveillance /sɜːˈveɪləns/	n.	the act of carefully watching a person suspected of a crime or a place where a crime may be committed （对犯罪嫌疑人或可能发生犯罪的地方的）监视
hobbyist /ˈhɒbiɪst/	n.	(formal) a person who is very interested in a particular hobby （业余）爱好者
quest /kwest/	n.	(formal, or literary) a long search for sth., especially for some quality such as happiness (~ for sth.) 探索，寻找，追求（幸福等）
component /kəmˈpəʊnənt/	n.	one of several parts of which sth. is made 组成部分，成分，部件
alternative /ɔːlˈtɜːnətɪv/	a.	(also alternate especially in North American English) that can be used instead of sth. else 可供替代的

analogy /ə'nælədʒɪ/	n.	a comparison of one thing with another thing that has similar features; a feature that is similar (~ between A and B; ~ with sth.) 类比，比拟，比喻	
elaborate /ɪ'læbərət/	a.	very complicated and detailed; carefully prepared and organized 复杂的，详尽的，精心制作的	
undertake /ˌʌndə'teɪk/	v.	to make yourself responsible for sth. and start doing it 承担，从事，负责	
optimal /'ɒptɪməl/	a.	most desirable possible under a restriction expressed or implied 最佳的，最优的，最理想的	

Exercise 1. Language: Match the words from Column A with those from Column B.

Column A	Column B
1. optimal	A. for happiness
2. alternative	B. technique
3. undertake	C. price
4. decision	D. making
5. surveillance	E. development
6. quest	F. decision
7. sturdy	G. options
8. product	H. research
9. marketing	I. choice
10. multiple	J. foundation

Exercise 2. Knowledge: Answer the following questions briefly according to the above article.

1. What is the purpose of conducting a marketing research?

   _____

2. Is an effective research always an elaborate one? Why?

   _____
   _____

3. Why does the author compare marketing research to the foundation of marketing research making?

   _____

4. Is it necessary for marketers to undertake all marketing researches by themselves?

   _____

5. If a marketer intends to undertake a research to know more about the company's product, what aspects of the product can he investigate into?

   _____

6. If a marketer plans to conduct a research to know more about the effectiveness of the company's promotion, what aspects can he investigate into?

   _____

7. If a company decides to find out more about its target market, what items does it need to know?

   _____

8. What research can benefit the company in terms of fixing a price for its new product?

   _____

Text B: Intensive Reading

Learning Resources

Marketing Research and Its Process

Marketing Research

Marketing research is the **systematic** collecting, recording and analysis of either qualitative or quantitative data about issues **pertaining** to marketing products and services. It is often used to identify and define marketing SWOT; generate, refine, and control marketing actions; monitor and evaluate marketing performance.

Marketing research is also used to identify and assess how changing elements of the marketing mix impacts consumer behaviors. The term is used interchangeably with market research by some researchers; however, experienced **practitioners** may still wish to draw a distinction between them, in that market research is concerned specifically with markets, while marketing research is concerned specifically about marketing processes.

The Process of Marketing Research

A typical marketing research process consists of 6 steps. The following is the general description of these steps.

Step 1: Problem Definition

The first step in any marketing research project is to define the problem. In defining the problem, the researcher should take into account the purpose of the study, the relevant background information, what information is needed, and how it will be used in decision making. Problem definition involves discussion with decision makers, interviews with industry experts or gurus, analysis of secondary data, and perhaps, some qualitative research. Once the problem is precisely defined, the research can be designed and conducted properly.

Step 2: Development of an Approach to the Problem

Development of an approach to the problem includes **formulating** an objective or theoretical framework, analytical models, research questions, **hypotheses**, and identifying characteristics or factors that can influence the research design. This process is guided by discussions with management and industry experts, case studies and **simulations**, analysis of secondary data, qualitative research and **pragmatic** considerations.

Step 3: Research Design Formulation

A research design is a framework or **blueprint** for conducting the marketing research project. It details the procedures necessary for obtaining the required information, and its purpose is to design a study that will test the hypotheses of interest, determine possible answers to the research questions, and provide the information needed for decision making. Conducting **exploratory** research, precisely defining the variables, and designing appropriate **scales** to measure them are also a part of the research design. The issue of how the data should be obtained from the **respondents** (for example, either by a survey or an experiment) must be **addressed**. It is also necessary to design a **questionnaire** and a sampling plan to select respondents for the study.

More formally, formulating the research design involves the following steps:

(1) Secondary data analysis;
(2) Qualitative research;
(3) Methods of collecting quantitative data (survey, observation or experiment);
(4) Definition of the information needed;
(5) Measurement and scaling procedures;
(6) Questionnaire design;
(7) Sampling process and sample size;
(8) Plan of data analysis.

Step 4: Fieldwork or Data Collection

Data collection involves a field force or staff that operates either in the field, as in the case of personal interviewing (in-home, mall **intercept**, or computer-assisted personal interviewing), from an office by telephone (telephone or computer-assisted telephone interviewing), or through mail (traditional mail and mail **panel** surveys with pre-recruited households). Proper selection, training, supervision, and evaluation of the field force helps minimize data-collection errors.

Step 5: Data Preparation and Analysis

Data preparation includes editing, **coding**, transcribing, and verifying data. Each questionnaire or observation form is inspected, or edited, and, if necessary, corrected. Number or letter codes are assigned to represent each response to each question in the questionnaire. The data from the questionnaires are transcribed and input directly into the computer.

Verification ensures that the data from the original questionnaires have been accurately transcribed, while data analysis gives meaning to the data. **Univariate** techniques are used for analyzing data when there is a single measurement of each element or unit in the sample, or, if there are several measurements of each element. On the other hand, **multivariate** techniques are used for analyzing data when there are two or more measurements on each element and the variables are analyzed **simultaneously**.

Step 6: Report Preparation and Presentation

The entire project should be documented in a written report which addresses the specific research questions identified, describes the approach, the research design, data collection, and data analysis procedures adopted, and presents the results and the major findings. The findings should be presented in a comprehensible format so that they can be readily used in the decision-making process. In addition, an oral presentation should be made to management using tables, figures, and graphs to enhance clarity and visual impact.

For these reasons, interviews with experts are more useful in conducting marketing research for industrial firms and for products of a technical nature, where it is relatively easy to identify and approach the experts. This method is also helpful in situations where little information is available from other sources, as in the case of radically new products.

Notes

Secondary Data Analysis

Secondary data are data collected for some purpose other than the problem at hand. Primary data, on the other hand, are originated by the researcher for the specific purpose of addressing the research problem. Secondary data include information made available by business and government sources, commercial marketing research firms, and computerized databases. Secondary data are an economical and quick source of background information.

Qualitative Research

Information, industry experts, and secondary data may not be sufficient to define the research problem. Sometimes qualitative research must be undertaken to gain a qualitative understanding of the problem and its underlying factors. Qualitative research is unstructured, exploratory in nature, based on small samples, and may utilize popular qualitative techniques such as focus groups (group interviews), word association (asking respondents to indicate their first responses to stimulus words), and in-depth interviews (one-on-one interviews which probe the respondents' thoughts in detail). Other exploratory research techniques, such as pilot surveys with small samples of respondents, may also be undertaken.　(978 words)

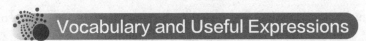

systematic /ˌsɪstəˈmætɪk/	*a.*	done according to a system or plan, in a thorough, efficient or determined way 成体系的，系统的，有条理的，有计划、有步骤的
pertain /pəˈteɪn/	*v.*	(formal) to be connected with sth./sb. 与……相关，关于
practitioner /prækˈtɪʃənə(r)/	*n.*	(formal) a person who regularly does a particular activity, especially one that requires skill 专门人才

hypothesis /haɪˈpɒθəsɪs/	*n.*	an idea or explanation of sth. that is based on a few known facts but that has not yet been proved to be true or correct（有少量事实依据但未被证实的）假说，假设
simulation /ˌsɪmjʊˈleɪʃn/	*n.*	a situation in which a particular set of conditions is created artificially in order to study or experience sth. that could exist in reality 模拟，仿真
pragmatic /præɡˈmætɪk/	*a.*	solving problems in a practical and sensible way rather than by having fixed ideas or theories 实用的，讲求实效的，务实的
blueprint /ˈbluːprɪnt/	*n.*	a plan which shows what can be achieved and how it can be achieved (~ for sth.) 行动方案，计划蓝图
exploratory /ɪkˈsplɒrətri/	*a.*	done with the intention of examining sth. in order to find out more about it 探索的，探究的
scale /skeɪl/	*n.*	a range of levels or numbers used for measuring sth. 等级，级别
respondent /rɪˈspɒndənt/	*n.*	a person who answers questions, especially in a survey 回答问题的人，（尤指）调查对象
address /əˈdres/	*v.*	(formal) to think about a problem or a situation and decide how you are going to deal with it (~ yourself to sth.) 设法解决，处理，对付
questionnaire /ˌkwestʃəˈneə(r)/	*n.*	a written list of questions that are answered by a number of people so that information can be collected from the answers (~ on/about sth.) 调查表，问卷
intercept /ˌɪntəˈsept/	*v.*	to stop sb./sth. that is going from one place to another from arriving 拦截，拦阻，截住
panel /ˈpænl/	*n.*	A panel is a small group of people who are chosen to do something, for example to discuss something in public or to make a decision. 专门小组
code /kəʊd/	*n.*	a system of words, letters, numbers or symbols that represent a message or record information secretly or in a shorter form 密码，代码
	v.	to write or print words, letters, numbers, etc. on sth. so that you know what it is, what group it belongs to, etc. 为……编码

univariate /ˌjuːnɪˈvɛərɪət/	a.	involving one variate or variable quantity 单变量的
multivariate /ˌmʌltɪˈvɛərɪət/	a.	involving two or more variable quantities 多变量的
simultaneously /ˌsɪməlˈteɪnɪəslɪ/	ad.	at the same time 同时地

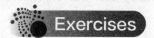

Exercises

Exercise 1. Language: Fill in the blanks with words of expressions from the above article.

1. In modern business competition, the _____ approach to business problems is often more successful than an idealistic one.
2. Marketing researchers have proposed an unproven _____ that the changes in consumer behavior may be attributed to global warming.
3. However, marketing management — specifically shifting market trends — are inherently _____, complex issues that are beyond one's ability to predict.
4. The researchers are experiencing a serious shortage of skilled hands, so they have to work on several projects _____.
5. An _____ survey is a research method used to gather on-site feedback from an audience, for example, you can stop a passer-by on the street and ask him questions to collect responses.
6. A research _____ is a group of people you have selected to take part in your survey research.
7. As the name implies, _____ research is an approach to market investigation that seeks to answer questions about a previously unknown subject through independent exploration.
8. Your marketing research report does not _____ the real issues that haunt marketers in recent years.
9. The survey _____ is allowed to designate up to five marketing opportunities that may be of greatest concern to his/her organization.
10. A business _____ is a strategic plan that tells those operating the business the productivity requirements, the necessary jobs, the milestones, the targets, and the expected outcomes.

Exercise 2. Knowledge: True or false statements. If the following statements are true, write T; if false, write F.

1. Marketing research is dedicated to the understanding of issues concerning the market. ( )

2. Market research is conducted to understand more about marketing as a process. （　）
3. Marketing research is mostly about conducting qualitative analysis of the issues pertaining to products and services. （　）
4. The marketing research plan can be designed before defining the research problem. （　）
5. In a formal process, a secondary data analysis should be conducted before designing a research plan. （　）
6. Developing a theoretical framework is one aspect of developing an approach to the research problem. （　）
7. A research hypothesis can be formulated on the basis of researcher's previous observations of the market phenomenon that cannot be satisfactorily explained by current theories. （　）
8. Marketing researchers rely on secondary data for the purpose of obtaining background information. （　）
9. Focus group, as a marketing research technique, can be adopted to gain a qualitative understanding of the problem and its underlying factors. （　）
10. Qualitative research is a structured and exploratory one to gain understanding of the research question. （　）

Exercise 3. Knowledge: Match the words from Column A with those from Column B.

Column A	Column B
1. research	A. collection
2. multivariate	B. model
3. analytical	C. question
4. pragmatic	D. factors
5. sample	E. framework
6. data	F. technique
7. theoretical	G. size
8. problem	H. definition
9. underlying	I. research
10. exploratory	J. considerations

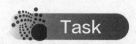

Oral practice: Work with your partners. Take turns to retell the process of conducting a typical marketing research to each other.

Following are some materials for your reference.

Tables and Figures

Tables

Tables can be described as text or numbers in the form of columns. They can be called a grid which has rows and columns with information or numbers. Every column has a heading or title. They are basically used to represent the compiled data in a simple form; they are not used to show relationship between separate values. Tables are denoted by Roman numerals as Table 7.1. While labeling the table, the label or numbers are centered and written on the top of the tables.

Table 7.1 Sample table showing decked heads and p value note

Variable	Visual		Infrared		F	β
	M	SD	M	SD		
Row 1	3.6	.49	9.2	1.02	69.9***	.12
Row 2	2.4	.67	10.1	.08	42.7***	.23
Row 3	1.2	.78	3.6	.46	53.9***	.34
Row 4	0.8	.93	4.7	.71	21.1***	.45

***$p<.01$.

Figures

Figures are any illustrations other than tables. They could be drawings, photos, bar charts, clip art, etc. Figures also include graphs and pie charts. Figures or graphs are used to illustrate the relationship between different data or different relationship patterns.

Tables and figures are chosen according to the most informative way to show the data. It also depends upon what data one is trying to display. Figures are denoted by Arabic numerals like Figure 7.1. The figures are labeled at the bottom.

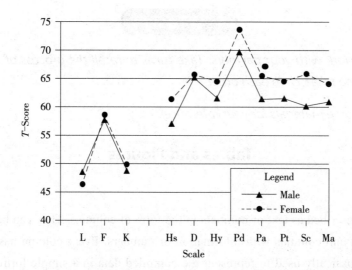

Figure 7.1 Mean MMPI validity and selected clinical scales scores for male alcoholics (n=637) and female alcoholics (n=339)

Summary

(1) Tables are text or numbers in the form of columns whereas figures are illustrations of different kinds like a pie chart, a drawing, a photograph, any graphic which represents the data in a graphic form.

(2) Tables are not used to represent any patterns of relationship whereas figures are used to show relationship patterns.

Text C: Extensive Reading

Learning Resources

Qualitative Methods in Marketing Research

Qualitative research explores consumers' ideas, perceptions and behaviors in depth with a relatively small number of research participants. It aims to answer questions with more complex, open-ended responses such as, "What does this mean to you…?" or "Why do you believe…?" or "How do you like to...?"

Qualitative research doesn't yield data that can be easily tabulated and translated into tidy percentages. Instead, it provides information that can help marketers understand the big picture of how customers perceive or experience something. Qualitative research techniques tend to be loosely structured, or unstructured and less formal, since the topical exploration may head in very different directions. These techniques can provide great insights to marketers, but because they involve relatively few participants, the results can be very subjective and idiosyncratic.

Often marketing research projects start with qualitative research activities to get a more complete picture of an issue or problem and how customers/consumers are thinking about it. They then follow up with a quantitative research that provides more specificity about what proportion of the population shares common preferences, beliefs, or behaviors. This information provides insights to help marketers refine their segmentation and targeting strategy, the marketing mix, or other considerations related to marketing effectiveness.

Typical qualitative methods include behavioral observation, in-depth interviews, focus groups, and social listening. Each of these methods is described below.

Observation

Marketers watch their customers and non-customers engage in a variety of behaviors. Examples include information-gathering, shopping, purchasing, product returns, complaints, and so forth. Observation can be as simple as a local fast-food restaurant manager watching the expression on customers' faces as they eat a new sandwich.

In-depth Interviews

In-depth interviews give marketing researchers the opportunity to delve deeply into topics of interest with the individuals they want to understand better. Research projects that use this method typically involve a fairly small number of these interviews, and they target the precise characteristics of the audiences that researchers want to understand. For example, a pharmaceutical company might want to understand a medical doctor's reasoning when considering which drugs to prescribe for certain medical conditions. Therefore the researchers conduct in-depth interviews with the doctors one by one, asking them some questions in order to explore deeper into the true reasons.

Focus Groups

Focus groups are much like in-depth interviews, except that they involve small groups (usually 6–12 individuals) rather than one person at a time. Like in-depth interviews, focus groups also try to delve deeply into topics of interest with people whose perspectives the researchers want to understand better. But unlike in-depth interviews, focus groups tend to be longer, running 60–90 minutes. Focus groups have the added benefit of inviting peers to talk to one another about the topics in question, so the researchers hear not just one individual's views but also listen to and observe the group's interactions.

Social Listening

With the proliferation of social media comes a tremendous opportunity to learn exactly what key individuals are saying with regard to marketing-related messages. Social listening is a systematic process for tracking what is being said about a given topic in forums such as Facebook, LinkedIn and blogs. When they engage in social listening, marketers monitor and analyze both positive and negative perspectives. Social listening helps marketers map not only who is saying what, but also who is influencing whom to help shape these opinions. (562 words)

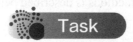

Writing: Just imagine your company, a mainstream provider of sportswear to young people, wants to find out the recent drop in its major products: the sports jerseys made with new materials. In order to find out the factors that lead to changes of consumer behavior, a qualitative research is needed.

Please suggest on the qualitative research method or a combination of methods that you may adopt. Further, write down what will you do and what questions are you going to ask and what do you expect from the research.

Word limit: 500 words.

Following are some examples for your reference.

Qualitative Research Examples

McDonald's

When conducting qualitative market research, McDonald's asks the customers several critical questions regarding best-performing products, the most appropriate pricing, the effective advertisements, and the most attended restaurants. Finding answers to these questions allows for analyzing whether the company managed to expand its customer base.

Furthermore, McDonald's collects customer feedback to improve the products. In particular, many customers were disappointed with the lack of healthy and organic options on the menu. As a result, the company added apple slices and other healthy items to the menu and launched an advertising campaign to show that chicken nuggets and burgers were made of real meat.

Starbucks

Starbucks encourages customers to share feedback on the official site and contribute ideas via Twitter. The company monitors social media, tracks cultural trends, and offers customers to test the products in the stores. From 2008 to 2018, Starbucks used the My Starbucks Idea platform to collect ideas and continuously improve its products. The company implemented over 275 consumer ideas, including recommendations about new products and methods to improve corporate responsibility.

Unit 8

New Product Development

Quote of the Unit:

"Be stubborn on vision but flexible on details."

—Jeff Bezos, Amazon

Learning Objectives:

1. Understand key concepts and process of new product development.
2. Understand the language used to describe the process of new product development.
3. Use both the language and knowledge learned to present your ideas concerning NPD issues.

Pre-class Questions:

1. According to your understanding, why is it necessary to keep developing new products?
2. Do you know how many steps does it take to develop a new product?
3. In your opinion, what is the most critical part when it comes to developing a new product?
4. In order to develop a product that will be successful in the marketing, what do developers need to consider seriously?

Unit 8 New Product Development

Text A: Lead-in

How to Develop a New App

Learning Resources

Let's imagine you're creating a brand new meal delivery App with some unique features that aren't available anywhere. Here's how you may go through several steps to develop it:

Step 1: You come up with an idea to create a food delivery App. There are already many food delivery Apps available in the market, but you plan to include two unique features that don't currently exist in your new App.

First, you want to add a quick-purchase option for people who are too hungry to think. All they need to do is input their address and budget, and the App will automatically order something with fast delivery time, and falls within their price range. Second, a **dietary** restriction setting that automatically removes meals containing **ingredients** you're **allergic** to, or foods that your religious belief forbids you from eating.

Step 2: This idea passes your proof of concept check, and your designers and engineers agree that only the first feature is possible. Restricting meals according to dietary needs would require too much work to be **feasible**, especially with so many partners.

Step 3: With one feature remaining, it's time to develop a specific concept. Your concept behind your app is to take the pain out of meal delivery. Instead of picking and choosing different meals from multiple menus, it's all taken care of with the click of a button. It's perfect for people that: (1) are in a rush; (2) families or groups of friends who can never decide what to eat; (3) people who don't care what they order.

Step 4: You and your team members attempt seriously to find out a possible marketing strategy for this new App.

Step 5: After **crunching** the numbers and **devising** a marketing strategy, you decide that your product can be developed and provide positive **ROI**.

Step 6: You successfully create and test various **prototypes** before finalizing your design.

Step 7: Before pulling the trigger and publishing your App, you alpha and beta test your product, uncovering some **user interface** issues which must be fixed before **proceeding**. After some fine-tuning, you're happy with the results and proceed to the final step.

Step 8: It's time to introduce your brand new meal delivery App with a unique feature to the market.

Conclusion: During each step of the new product development model, your focus should always be on producing greater customer value and innovation, as that's how you'll ensure your product is a success. (414 words)

Vocabulary and Useful Expressions

dietary /ˈdaɪətərɪ/	a.	related to anything that concerns a person's diet 饮食的，有关饮食的
ingredient /ɪnˈgriːdɪənt/	n.	one of the things from which sth. is made, especially one of the foods that are used together to make a particular dish 成分,（尤指烹饪）原料
allergic /əˈlɜːdʒɪk/	a.	having an allergy to sth. (~ to sth.) （对……）过敏的
feasible /ˈfiːzəbl/	a.	that is possible and likely to be achieved 可行的，行得通的
crunch /krʌntʃ/	v.	to do a lot of calculations using a calculator or computer （用计算器或计算机大量地）处理（数字）
devise /dɪˈvaɪz/	v.	to invent sth. new or a new way of doing sth. 发明，设计，想出
ROI		return on investment 投资回报
prototype /ˈprəʊtətaɪp/	n.	the first design of sth. from which other forms are copied or developed (~ for/of sth.) 原型，雏形，最初形态
user interface		(computer science) a program that controls a display for the user (usually on a computer monitor) and that allows the user to interact with the system （计算机）用户界面
proceed /prəˈsiːd/	v.	to continue doing sth. that has already been started; to continue being done (~ with sth.) 继续做（或从事、进行）

Exercises

Exercise 1. Language: Can you suggest some names for these different steps of developing a new product?

Unit 8 New Product Development

Step 1: _____
Step 2: _____
Step 3: _____
Step 4: _____
Step 5: _____
Step 6: _____
Step 7: _____
Step 8: _____

Exercise 2. Knowledge: Which step do you think is the most critical one in the whole process of developing a new product? Share your ideas and justify briefly.

Among these 8 steps, I think the _____ step is the most important. Because:
_____
_____
_____
_____

Text B: Intensive Reading

Learning Resources

An 8-step New Product Development Process

A company must keep developing new products or modifying current products to differentiate and remain competitive in the market. New products are often developed to replace the old ones, to diversify the product line, or to enrich the product mix.

In the following sections, we will mainly explore an 8-step new product development process.

Step 1: Idea Generation

The whole process starts with idea generation. Idea generation refers to the systematic search for new product ideas. Typically, a company generates hundreds of ideas before selecting a handful of best product ideas. People often use two sources of new ideas.

115

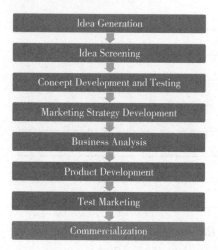

Internal sources: the company finds new ideas internally through formal research and development (R&D). They need to identify customer demands and understand customer needs through market research. Many companies encourage internal brainstorming **sessions** to come up with workable ideas. They often provide incentives for employees who are engaged in these activities.

External sources: marketers can collect information and ideas from all kinds of external sources, including distributors, suppliers and even competitors. But the most important external source is the customer, because the new product development process should focus on creating customer values.

Remember that this phase does not suggest generating a foolproof plan for the new product and implementing it. You can have **unproven** ideas that can be filtered or **screened** later after the discussion. Here are some suggestions on how to initiate the search for new ideas:

(1) Highlight on the customer problems;
(2) Analyze each of the listed problems;
(3) Identify their possible solutions;
(4) Come up with the final problem statement and solution.

Step 2: Idea Screening

Idea screening is defined as evaluating and contrasting new product ideas to get the most promising ones for business. While idea generation is to create as many ideas as possible, the purpose of the following stages is to reduce that number significantly. The reason is simple: the company only wants product ideas that it has enough resources to develop and that will very possibly be turned into profitable products.

The general criteria for idea screening include product **viability**, technical **feasibility** and profitability. Product viability means the new product idea should be able to survive in the market. Technical feasibility means that there should be techniques that can help realize product ideas. The last one, profitability means even if the techniques are available, the company should examine the cost of manufacturing and selling the new product, whether it is profitable to do so.

Step 3: Concept Development and Testing

After selecting the best ideas, it is time to develop product concepts based on the ideas. A product concept can be understood as a detailed version of the new product idea stated in meaningful consumer terms.

Imagine a car manufacturer like Chery plans to develop an electric car. The marketer's task now is to develop this new product idea into alternative product concepts. Then, the company can find out how appealing or attractive each concept is to customers and choose the best one. Possible product concepts for this electric car could be:

Concept 1: a mid-sized car with affordable price, designed as a second family car to be used around town for visiting friends and doing shopping;

Concept 2: a mid-priced sporty compact car appealing to young singles and couples;

Concept 3: a high-end mid-sized sports utility vehicle (SUV) appealing to those who like the space SUVs provide but also want an economical car.

As we can see, these concepts need to be quite precise in order to be meaningful and understandable by customers.

Concept Testing

Once new product concepts are developed, they need to be tested with groups of target consumers. The concepts can be presented to consumers either symbolically or physically. The question is always: does the concept have strong consumer appeal? For some concept tests, a word or picture description might be enough. However, to increase the reliability of the test, a more concrete and physical presentation of the product concept may be needed.

After exposing the concept to the group of target consumers, they will be asked to answer questions in order to find out the level of consumer appeal and customer value of each concept.

Step 4: Marketing Strategy Development

When concept testing, it is time to design an initial marketing strategy for the new product based on the product concept for introducing this new product to the market.

The marketing strategy statement mainly consists of three parts and should be formulated carefully: a description of the target market, the planned value proposition, and the sales, market share and profit goals for the first few years; an outline of the product's planned price, distribution and marketing budget for the first year; the planned long-term sales, profit goals and the marketing mix strategy.

Besides, it also describes how to penetrate the market, in other words, **route** to market:

whether to produce it by yourself or outsource the production.

Step 5: Business Analysis

Once a product concept and related marketing strategy are determined, marketers can evaluate the business attractiveness of the proposed new product. This involves a review of the sales, costs and profit projections for the new product to find out whether these factors satisfy the company's objectives. All the estimated sales and costs figure together can eventually be used to analyse the new product's financial attractiveness. If they turn out to be financially attractive, then it is time to go on to the product development stage.

Step 6: Product Development

If the product concept passes the business test, it must be developed into a physical product, to ensure that the product idea can be turned into a physical and workable market offering.

The R&D department will develop and test one or more physical versions of the product concept. Developing a successful prototype, however, can take days, weeks, months or even years, depending on the product and prototype methods.

Also, products often undergo tests to make sure they perform safely and effectively. This can be done by the firm itself or outsourced to third-party companies.

In many cases, marketers involve actual customers in product testing. Consumers can evaluate prototypes and work with pre-release products.

Step 7: Test Marketing

In this stage, the product and its proposed marketing programme are tested in real market settings, but within a much smaller scale. Therefore, test marketing gives marketers experience with marketing the product before going to the great expense of full market introduction. In fact, it allows the company to test the product and its entire marketing programme, including targeting and positioning strategy, advertising, distributions, packaging, etc. before the full investment is made.

The amount of test marketing necessary varies with each new product. Especially when introducing a new product that requires a large investment, when the risks are high, or when the firm is not sure of the product or its marketing programme, a lot of test marketing may be carried out.

Step 8: Commercialization

If the company receives positive feedback from test marketing, it will very probably go on to the final stage: **commercialization**. Commercialization is the process of introducing a new product or production method into commerce — making it available on the market. In the case of a major new consumer product, it may spend hundreds of millions of dollars for advertising, sales promotion, and other marketing efforts in the first year. For instance, to introduce the Surface series, Microsoft spent nearly $400 million on an advertising blitz through TV, print, radio, outdoor, the Internet, events, public relations, and sampling.

The company may have to face the problem of whether to launch the new product in a single location, a region, the national market, or the international market simultaneously. Normally, companies don't have the confidence, capital and capacity to launch new products into full national or international distribution once and for all. Instead, they usually develop a planned market **roll-out** over time. Take Apple Inc. as an example, it launches its latest iPhone in multiple stages, each consists of several countries in the world.   (1341 words)

Vocabulary and Useful Expressions

session /ˈseʃn/	n.	A session of a particular activity is a period of that activity. （某项活动的）一段时间，一场，一节
unproven /ˌʌnˈpruːvn/	a.	not proved or tested 未验证的，未经检验的
screen /skriːn/	v.	to check sth. to see if it is suitable or if you want it 审查，筛选
viability /ˌvaɪəˈbɪlətɪ/	n.	the ability to continue to exist or develop (as a product, for example) 生存能力
feasibility /ˌfiːzəˈbɪlɪtɪ/	n.	the possibility and likeliness to be achieved 可行性
route /ruːt/	n.	a particular way of achieving sth. (~ to sth.) 途径，渠道
commercialization /kəˌmɜːʃəlaɪˈzeɪʃn/	n.	the act of commercializing something; involving something in commerce 商品化
roll-out /ˈrəʊlˌaʊt/	n.	an occasion when a company introduces or starts to use a new product 新产品发布会，新产品的推出

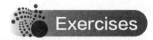

Exercise 1. Language: Fill in the blanks with words or expressions from the above article.

1. _____ is the process that allows businesses to raise and solve problems of new products and bring them to the market.
2. A market _____ often refers to a significant product release, which is frequently accompanied by a strong marketing campaign, to generate consumer interest.
3. A _____ serves to provide specifications for a real, working system rather than a theoretical one.
4. A _____ to market strategy, also known as a sales execution strategy provides a road-map for companies to get their products from the factory or warehouse to the end-users.
5. Many companies in Britain are keen on the idea of tax _____ for R&D.
6. Product _____ refers to the business potential of a specific product — that is, how relevant and interesting the product will be to target buyer personas.
7. Many people feel the technology is too new and _____, so they hesitate.
8. The process of evaluating ideas to drop as many ideas as possible from consideration is called idea _____.
9. During the brainstorming _____, people are encouraged to generate as many ideas as possible, regardless of their quality.
10. Marketers need to use estimated sales revenues and profits to analyze the new product's financial _____.

Exercise 2. Knowledge: True or false statements. If the following statements are true, write T; if false, write F.

1. Idea generation is the starting point of the whole NPD process, it is also the start of systemic search for new product. ( )
2. Product concepts should be presented in physical form. ( )
3. Outsourcing production, which is known as OEM, is one route to market. ( )
4. Prototype is only a nonoperational model for observational purposes. ( )
5. When it is time to conduct business analysis, a review of the sales, costs and profit projections for the new product is necessary. ( )
6. The business attractiveness of the new product can be projected on the basis of estimated costs, sales revenues and profits. ( )
7. Only new product developers are involved in product testing. ( )
8. In test marketing, the new product and its proposed marketing programme are tested in

virtual market settings to test the possible effects. ( )
9. Safety test of the prototype can be outsourced to third party companies. ( )
10. The common criteria for idea screening include product viability, technical feasibility and profitability. ( )

Exercise 3. Knowledge: Answer the following questions briefly according to the above article.

1. What are the major sources of new product ideas in the idea generation stage?

2. What questions can marketers ask to help come up with new product ideas?

3. What is the purpose of conducting idea screening? How can developers screen the ideas more effectively?

4. As for route to market, how many routes can you think of?

5. Commercialization seems to be the final stage of new product development process, but is it really the end?

Oral practice: In order to collect enough new product ideas, in the idea generation stage, developers often resort to brainstorming for generating as many ideas as possible. Work with your partners to find out the typical procedure and rules governing a brainstorming session. Discuss and justify why a brainstorming session should be organized and conducted in that way. You are encouraged to use both the language and knowledge learned in this unit.

Text C: Extensive Reading

Successful New Product Development Cases

Learning Resources

New products are the lifeblood of any business — they allow companies to constantly evolve to better satisfy customers' needs and expectations, increase their market share, and gain a definite advantage over competitors.

Yet of thousands of products entering the market each year, it is estimated that around 70%–80% of them fail. Careful planning is essential to minimize risks and increase the odds of success, and this can only happen when a company has a solid product development strategy in place.

Successful companies rely on well-defined product development strategies to organize user and market research, understand their customers' pain points and expectations, and accurately plan the resources and time required to develop the product.

Below are two successful product development examples from two hi-tech companies. Learn how they deliver superior value to customers, innovate, and boost growth while keeping the customer at the center of their new product development process.

The Case of Amazon

Jeff Bezos started Amazon as an online bookstore in 1994. Since its inception, the company expanded to become the world's largest online marketplace, AI assistant provider, live-streaming platform, and cloud computing platform. But what's the secret behind Amazon's worldwide success?

Amazon developed a set of scalable and repeatable processes, combined with 14 leadership principles that the company uses every day, from discussing ideas for new projects to deciding on the best approach to solving a problem.

The first Amazon leadership principle and the most important one is customer obsession: leaders start with the customer and work backwards. They work vigorously to earn and maintain customer trust. Although leaders pay attention to competitors, they obsess over customers.

It's no surprise that Amazon's product development strategy and approach focus entirely on customer needs.

The Amazon Working Backward Method

Amazon's approach to product development is called "working backward". Rather than starting with an idea for a new feature, product, or line of business, Amazon starts from the customer experience and works backward from that.

The first step in the product development process is to write an internal press release announcing the launch of the new product. Press releases are centered around the existing customer problem, why current solutions fail to correct the problem, and how the new product would blow away existing solutions.

If product managers find it hard to write a press release or understand why a product would add value to customers, this means the product isn't worth the effort. They will need to continue to refine the document until they develop ideas that will generate value.

Once the project moves into development, the team can use the press release as a strategic guide. This document serves a similar function as the product roadmap — it keeps team members on the same page and acts as an overview of the product's direction, priorities, and progress.

The Case of Zoom

Zoom is a cloud-based conferencing tool that allows users to virtually interact with each other through audio, video, and chat. Founded in 2011 by Eric Yuan and launched in 2013, Zoom became synonymous with video conferencing. In response to COVID-19, Zoom was recognized as Frost & Sullivan's Company of the Year for 2020 and one of the best tools for product managers at the 2020 Product Award.

Customer Focus

Eric Yuan, founder and CEO of Zoom: "From the moment we founded Zoom, our main focus has been to provide a cloud video communications solution that would make customers happy. That focus has continued to guide all our innovations, partnerships, and other initiatives."

Zoom's product strategy revolves around customers' needs. Customers are at the center of all business and product development decisions. This principle is what inspired Eric Yuan to found Zoom in the first place.

Before founding Zoom in 2011, Eric Yuan worked as VP of Engineering at the video start-up Webex, then acquired by Cisco. By engaging with consumers, he observed that users were dissatisfied with the existing video collaboration solutions. Inspired to solve user needs, Eric decided to found Zoom and build a video conferencing tool that worked, was simple to use, and cost-effective.

During the years, the company has continued to expand its customer focus model. The team listens carefully to product feedback and acts on it to fine-tune the product and deliver better user experiences.

Product-led Growth

Zoom is an excellent example of product-led growth — a business methodology in which user acquisition, expansion, conversion, and retention are driven primarily by the product itself. Zoom offers a hassle-free and simple connection to its customers. The platform and its core features are entirely free for up to 100 participants and a maximum of 40 minutes. In this way, users can experience the product, invite others to try it out, or upgrade to a paid plan.

"This market is extremely crowded. Without a freemium product, I think you're going to lose the opportunity to let many users test your products," explains Eric Yuan in an interview. "We make our freemium product work so well. That's why almost every day there are so many users coming to our website. If they like our product, very soon they are going to pay for the subscription."

Flexibility

Zoom's success is also due to its ability to adapt its product strategy to the changing market conditions. When the COVID-19 pandemic hit in early 2020, video conferencing tools became the norm for business calls, school lessons, and catching up with friends and family. Following a surge in user demand, Zoom partnered with Oracle Cloud to support infrastructure capabilities and doubled down on security and privacy improvements. The company also prioritized education, teaching its new users how to use the tool for teaching, working remotely, or meeting friends and family.   (953 words)

(**Source:** https://maze.co/collections/product-development/examples/.)

Writing: After reading the two cases above, combined with content from Text A and Text B, think about what may be the most essential and important part of developing a new product. You can also search for ideas from other references books or online content to aid your thinking and writing. Then write down your ideas. You are expected to use both the knowledge and language learned in this unit, to make your writing reasonable, readable and logical.

Word limit: 300 words.

Unit 9

Product Life Cycle

English for Marketing

🔔 *Quote of the Unit:*

"Good companies manage engineering. Great companies manage product."

—Thomas Schranz, founder and CEO of Blossom

🔔 *Learning Objectives:*

1. Understand the definition of product life cycle (PLC).
2. Understand the four stages of PLC and their characteristics.
3. Master the language used to describe the stages of PLC.
4. Apply the PLC model to analyze products, and express it in the language learned in this unit.

🔔 *Pre-class Questions:*

1. Have you ever observed the nature and found out the life cycle of any particular animals or plants?
2. Can you briefly describe the life cycle of human beings? Which stage are you currently in?
3. If we compare a product to a living creature, what stages of life cycle must it go through?

Text A: Lead-in

Product Life Cycle Examples

Learning Resources

The product life cycle **curve consists** of four key stages. A product must firstly go through the introduction stage before passing into the growth stage where it enjoys rapid growth of sales volume and market share. Next it proceeds to the maturity stage and eventually arrives at the decline stage, which is the final stage of its life cycle. The following examples illustrate these stages in more detail.

3D televisions: 3D technology may have been around for a few decades. But only after **considerable** investment from broadcasters and hi-tech companies that makes it possible for 3D TV sets to be available for the home. That provides a good example of a product that is in the introduction stage.

Blue-ray players: With advanced technology delivering superb viewing experience, including extremely high-quality pictures and sound effects, blue-ray equipment is currently enjoying a steady increase in sales and market share, which **exemplifies** a product in the growth stage.

DVD players: Introduced two decades ago, manufacturers that make DVDs and the equipment needed to play them, have established a strong market share. However, they still have to deal with the challenges from other technologies. This is a typical example of a product in the maturity stage.

Video recorders: While it is still possible to purchase VCRs, this is a product that is definitely in the decline stage, as it's become easier and cheaper for consumers to **switch** to the other, more modern formats. In other words, VCR is no longer popular with the consumers.

Another example within the consumer electronics sector also shows the **emergence** and growth of new technologies, and what could be the beginning of the end for those that have been around for some time.

Holographic projection: Only recently introduced into the market, holographic projection technology allows consumers to turn any flat surface into a touchscreen **interface**. With a huge investment in research and development, and high prices that will only appeal to early adopters, this is another good example of the first stage of the product life cycle.

Tablet PCs: There are a growing number of tablet PC for consumers to choose from, as this product passes through the growth stage of the cycle and more competitors start to rush into a market that really developed after the launch of Apple's iPad.

Laptops: Laptop computers have been around for a number of years, but more advanced components, as well as diverse features that appeal to different segments of the market, will help **sustain** this product as it passes through the maturity stage.

Typewriters: Typewriters, and even electronic word processors, have very limited **functionality**. With consumers demanding a lot more from the electronic equipment they buy, typewriter is a type of product that is passing through the final stage of the product life cycle.

While it's usually left up to the manufacturers and their marketers to worry about product life cycle management and what implications the different stages might have for their business, considering actual products is also a good way to show consumers the part they play in this life cycle. (515 words)

(**Source:** https://productlifecyclestages.com/product-life-cycle-examples/.)

Vocabulary and Useful Expressions

curve /kɜːv/	n.	a line or surface that bends gradually; a smooth bend 曲线
consist /kənˈsɪst/	v.	to be formed from the things or people mentioned (~ of) 由……组成（或构成）
considerable /kənˈsɪdərəbl/	a.	(formal) great in amount, size, importance, etc. 相当多（或大、重要等）的
exemplify /ɪɡˈzemplɪfaɪ/	v.	to be a typical example of sth. 是……的典型（或典范、榜样）
switch /swɪtʃ/	v.	to change or make sth. change from one thing to another (~ sth. over/ from sth. to sth.; ~ between A and B) （使）改变，转变，突变
emergence /ɪˈmɜːdʒəns/	n.	the emergence of something is the process or event of its coming into existence 出现，兴起
holographic /ˌhɒləˈɡræfɪk/	a.	connected with holograms 全息图的
interface /ˈɪntəfeɪs/	n.	(computing) the way a computer program presents information to a user or receives information from a user, in particular the layout of the screen and the menus （人机）界面（尤指屏幕布局和菜单）

sustain /sə'steɪn/   *v.*   to make sth. continue for some time without becoming less; to provide enough of what sb./sth. needs in order to live or exist 使保持，使稳定持续，维持（生命、生存）

functionality /ˌfʌŋkʃə'nælətɪ/   *n.*   the range of functions that a computer or other electronic system can perform 功能，功能性

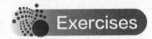

Exercise 1. Knowledge: Answer the following questions according to your knowledge or experience and discuss with your partners.

1. The article says 3D TV is in the introduction stage, which means it is yet to be well accepted or popular. Is this statement real? If not, what is the fact?

   _____

2. The article mentions that blue-ray players are currently picking up sales so it is in the growth stage. Consider the situation in Chinese market, is it real that blue-ray equipment is becoming an increasingly popular item? If not, then what is the truth?

   _____

3. The article picks DVD player as a product in its maturity stage, which implies the market is already saturated with DVD players from different competitors. But is it the real case in Chinese market? If not, then what is the truth?

   _____

Exercise 2. Language: Fill in the blanks with words or expressions from the above article.

1. The new product is significantly more compact than any comparable laptop, with no loss in _____.

2. The new law would encourage companies to _____ from coal and oil to other cleaner fuels.

3. The failed new product development project wasted a _____ amount of time and money.

4. The _____ of new technologies has prompted the development of futuristic products.

5. The diagram shows each firm will face a downward-sloping demand _____.

6. On the basis of a massive amount of customer feedback, the company has decided to

proceed to the development of better user _____ in order to improve user satisfaction.

7. The architect tries to use the interior design of this room to _____ his ideal of minimalism and practicality.

Oral practice: Can you provide an example of a series of related products that are in different stages of their PLC?

For your reference:
(1) hookah（水烟）
(2) cigar
(3) cigarette
(4) electronic cigarette

Text B: Intensive Reading

Product Life Cycle

Learning Resources

When we talk about life cycle, we normally refer to the human life cycle: from birth to **adolescence**, then adulthood, till the later age, and at last, death.

Similarly, a product can also be regarded as having a life cycle. We are now talking about a product, but what is a product?

Here we define product as anything that satisfies a consumer's need. It may be a tangible product: paper, clothes, toys, cars, and houses; or an intangible service: banking, health care, **hospitality** service, airline service, etc.

Irrespective of the kind of product, all products introduced into the market undergo a common life cycle. To understand what this product life cycle theory is all about, let us have a quick look at its definition: A product life cycle refers to the time period between the launch of a product into the market till it is finally withdrawn from the market.

In a nutshell, product life cycle or PLC is an **odyssey** from being new and innovative to being old and outdated. This cycle is split into four different stages which **encompass** the product's journey from its entry to exit from the market.

As shown in Figure 9.1, this cycle is based on the familiar biological life cycle wherein a seed is planted (the introduction stage), germinates, sends out roots in the ground, and shoots with branches and leaves against **gravity** (the growth stage), thereby maturing into an adult (the maturity stage). As the plant lives its life and nears old age, it **shrivels** up, shrinks and dies out (the decline stage).

Figure 9.1 The biological life cycle

Similarly, a product also has a life cycle of its own. A product's entry or launching phase into the market corresponds to the introduction stage. As the product gains popularity and wins the trust of consumers it begins to grow. Further, with increasing sales, the product captures enough market share and becomes stable in the market. This is called the maturity stage.

However, after some time the product gets **overshadowed** by latest technological developments and entry of superior competitors in the market. Soon the product becomes **obsolete** and needs to be withdrawn from the market. This is the decline phase.

The graph of a product's life cycle just looks like a bell-shaped curve, as shown in Figure 9.2.

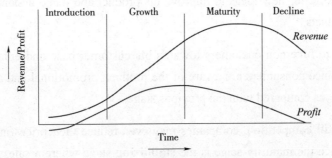

Figure 9.2 Product life cycle

Now let me show you some details of these four stages.

The first stage is the introduction stage. After conducting thorough market research, the company develops its product. Once the product is ready, a test market is carried out to check the viability of the product in the actual market before it can set foot into the mass market. Results of the test market are used to make correction if any and then the product is launched into the market with various promotional strategies.

Since the product has just been introduced, growth observed is minimal, market size is small and marketing costs are steep. Thus, introduction stage is an awareness creating stage, and is not associated with profits. Once the introduction stage goes as expected, the initial spark has been set. However, the fire has to be **kindled** carefully.

The marketer has managed to gain the consumer's attention and works on nurturing loyal customers. He also works on increasing his product's market share by investing in aggressive advertising and marketing plans. He will also use different promotional strategies like offering discounts, limited time offer, BOGO, etc. to increase sales.

As output increases, economies of scale are seen and better prices come about conducing to profits in this stage. The marketer maintains the quality and features of the product and seeks brand building. The aim here is to entice consumers to prefer and choose this product over those sold by competitors.

As sales increase, distribution channels are added and the product is marketed to a broader audience. Thus, rapid sales and profits are characteristics of this stage.

Maturity stage views the most competition as different companies struggle to maintain their respective market shares. The **cliché** "survival of the fittest" is applicable here.

Companies are busy monitoring product's value by the consumers and its sales generation. Most of the profits are made at this stage and research costs are minimum. Any research conducted will be confined to product enhancement and improvement alone. The manufacturer is constantly looking for new ideas to improve his product and make it stand out among the competitor's products.

His main aim is to **lure** non-customers towards his customer base and enlarge the existing customer base. Since consumers are aware of the product, promotional and advertising costs will also be lower as compared with the previous stage.

In the midst of **stiff** competition, companies may even reduce their prices in response to the tough times. Hence the maturity stage is the **stabilizing** stage wherein sales are high but the pace is slow. However, brand loyalty develops thereby making more profits.

After a period of stable growth, the revenue generated from sales of the product starts **dipping** due to market saturation, stiff competition and latest technological developments.

The consumer loses interest in the product and begins to seek other options. This stage is characterized by shrinking market share, dwindling product popularity and plummeting profits. And we call it decline stage.

This stage is a very delicate stage and needs to be handled wisely. The type of response contributes to the future of the product. The company needs to make special efforts to raise the product's popularity in the market once again either by reducing the cost of the product tapping new markets or withdrawing the product from the market. The manufacturer will cut down all non-profit distribution channels and continue focusing on improving the product design and features so as to gain back the lost customer base.

However, if this strategy fails the manufacturer will have no option but to withdraw the product from the market. It is important to note that not all products go through the entire life cycle. Just as how not all seeds sown can germinate, not all products launched into the market can succeed. Some fail in the introduction stage, while some cannot manage to capture market share due to quick failure.

Moreover, some marketers quickly change strategies when the product reaches decline phase and by various promotional strategies to regain the lost glory, thereby achieving cyclic maturity phases.

One more thing: there are no time frames for the stages. The growth stage for a product may take a very long time while the maturity stage may be extremely short. Application of product life cycle is important to marketers because via this analysis they can manage their product well and prevent it from incurring losses. A well-managed product life cycle leads to rise in profits and does not necessarily end. Product innovations, new marketing strategies, etc. keep the product appealing to customers for a very long period of time. (1167 words)

Vocabulary and Useful Expressions

| adolescence /ˌædəˈlesns/ | *n.* | the time in a person's life when he or she develops from a child into an adult 青春期，青春 |

hospitality /ˌhɒspɪˈtæləti/		n.	food, drink or services that are provided by an organization for guests, customers, etc. （款待客人、顾客等的）食物，饮料，服务 the hospitality industry (= hotels, restaurants, etc.) 招待性行业（如旅馆、饭店等）
odyssey /ˈɒdəsi/		n.	(literary) a long journey full of experiences 艰苦的跋涉，漫长而充满风险的历程
encompass /ɪnˈkʌmpəs/		v.	(formal) to include a large number or range of things 包含，包括，涉及（大量事物）
gravity /ˈɡrævəti/		n.	the force which causes things to drop to the ground 重力，万有引力
shrivel /ˈʃrɪvl/		v.	to become or make sth. dry and wrinkled as a result of heat, cold or being old [~ sth. (up)] （使）枯萎，干枯，皱缩
overshadow /ˌəʊvəˈʃædəʊ/		v.	to make sb./sth. seem less important, or successful 使显得逊色，使黯然失色
obsolete /ˈɒbsəliːt/		a.	no longer used because sth. new has been invented 淘汰的，废弃的，过时的
kindle /ˈkɪndl/		v.	to start burning; to make a fire start burning 开始燃烧，点燃
cliché /ˈkliːʃeɪ/		n.	a phrase or an idea that has been used so often that it no longer has much meaning and is not interesting 陈词滥调，陈腐的套语
lure /lʊə(r)/		v.	(disapproving) to persuade or trick sb. to go somewhere or to do sth. by promising them a reward 劝诱，引诱，诱惑
stiff /stɪf/		a.	more difficult or severe than usual 困难的，艰难的，严厉的，激烈的
stabilize /ˈsteɪbəlaɪz/		v.	to become or to make sth. become firm, steady and unlikely to change; to make sth. stable （使）稳定，稳固
dip /dɪp/		v.	to go downwards or to a lower level; to make sth. do this （使）下降，下沉

Unit 9   Product Life Cycle

1. in a nutshell: (to say or express something) in a very clear way, using few words   简而言之，用简明的话
2. economies of scale: the financial advantages that a company gains when it produces large quantities of products   规模经济，规模效应
3. in the midst of: while something is happening or being done; while you are doing sth.   当某事发生时，在某人做某事时
4. *shrinking* market share, *dwindling* product popularity and *plummeting* profits: these three verbs italicized are synonyms that refer to the drop or reduction of something

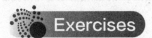

Exercise 1. Language: Fill in the blanks with words or expressions from the above article and translate the sentences into Chinese.

1. The company currently faces _____ competition from its rivals.

2. Sales for this quarter have _____ from 38.7 million to 33 million.

3. As the old _____ goes, fan is short for fanatic.

4. The older version of the product is definitely _____ by the latest edition.

5. Some major retailers are offering free Didi rides to _____ customers to get back into their doors.

6. The company's businesses _____ shipbuilding, life insurance, construction, hotels, amusement park operation and more.

135

7. Researchers often compare the process of new product development to an _____.

8. Face with serious inflation, the government tried very hard to _____ product prices.

9. This successful marketing case has helped _____ the imagination of generations of marketers.

10. Before adopting a new product idea, marketers need to carefully analyze the market _____ of it.

Exercise 2. Knowledge: Try to summarize the product life cycle in four sentences briefly.

1. Introduction: it is the period of time when...

2. Growth: it is the stage when...

3. Maturity: it refers to the situation where...

4. Decline: it symbolizes a stage when...

Exercise 3. Knowledge: True or false statements. If the following statements are true, write T; if false, write F.

1. Adolescence of human life cycle can be compared to as the growth stage in the product life cycle. ( )
2. A product can be defined as anything that can satisfy a consumer's particular need. ( )
3. When a product becomes obsolete in the market, it is about time to withdraw it from the market and replace it with a new one. ( )
4. As a product grows in the market, it gains more popularity and larger market share. ( )
5. The maturity stage refers to the situation when the product is becoming old and outdated. ( )
6. Economies of scale can help reduce manufacturer's average cost of production and hence

improve its competitiveness. ( )
7. The cliché "survival of the fittest" indicates that only if a product can outcompete its major rivals can it survive and develop in the market. ( )
8. During the maturity stage, the research and development cost is at its maximum. ( )
9. Product enhancement or improvement strategies can help companies lure more non-customers to try their products. ( )
10. Maturity stage is a time period when profit grows but the situation is not yet stable for the product. ( )

Oral practice: The product life cycle indicates the different stages a product should go through. Discuss with your partners, and suggest some measures to deal with products in these four different stages.

For example, if a product is in the introduction stage, what should be done to ensure its market acceptance? If a product is in the growth stage, what should be done to maintain its growth momentum? If a product is in its maturity stage, what should be done to maximize the benefits from selling it? If a product is in its decline stage, what measures should be taken to reduce the potential loss that it may incur?

Discuss and list some brief measures.

Text C: Extensive Reading

Learning Resources

The Product Life Cycle of iPod

Introduction Stage

Apple did not invent the MP3, it only made it mainstream and popular. Though being a late entrant in the MP3 market, the product caught the market's attention with its advanced capabilities, user-friendly click-wheel control, and most importantly, its "cool factor".

The first iPod launched were basic models having a memory of only 5GB and 10 GB and came with a hefty price tag of $399. However, Apple created a buzz for the MP3 player and its iPod through its brand awareness campaigns, informative television commercials demonstrating the benefits and utility of the iPod, and it also convinced the consumers that owning an iPod is a cool experience.

Growth Stage

Apple iPod's growth was mainly triggered by the launch of the iTunes Music Store in 2003 and progressive improvement in the hardware of the iPod.

Further, the iPod was offered in attractive colours, bigger storage and with additional features. The second and third generation of the iPod did face some competition from firms which targeted the iPod on its size and features.

The MP3 player was becoming one of the fastest growing consumer electronic product since its launch and gained market acceptance at an amazingly fast pace. Expanding the product line became critical as the innovator market was about to reach its point of saturation.

Apple launched the iPod Mini in 2004 to enhance its market appeal. The iPod Mini became a real heat among the students and women, mainly due to its small size, a wide range of color and lower pricing.

Apple introduced the iPod Nano, iPod Shuffle and the iPod Touch over the next three years to drive away the competition from MP3 players such as Samsung's YP-P2 and Microsoft Zune.

The further expansion of Apple Stores in the United Kingdom and the European Union in 2003 expanded the distribution reach of Apple's iPod which was limited to supermarkets and big box electronic stores.

During this period, Apple committed about 60 percent of its over advertising budget for the iPod, and by 2007, the Apple iPod had a mammoth market share in the MP3 market, with a market share of 72.7%.

And if you begin to see it as a marketer, these are exactly the characteristics of the growth stage of the product life cycle. Your product starts to sell like crazy, you spend more on it in terms of the marketing spend and it does capture a sizable market share.

Maturity Stage

The Apple iPod reached its maturity in 2008 with its global sales crossing 54 million units.

According to Michael Porter, a business can achieve competitive advantage in a mature market by adopting either of these three strategies, i.e. focus, product differentiation and cost leadership.

Apple maintained its market share during the maturity stage of product life cycle of Apple iPod by adopting the product differentiation strategy.

Apple continued to introduce new features in every new generation of the iPod and stayed a few steps ahead of its competition. Before the competition could imitate the existing iPod, Apple introduced another latest generation of the iPod with newer and many improved features.

This includes introducing color screens, video playback feature, camera, Nike+ integration, offering a higher battery life, and much more.

Apple continued to use the existing ecosystem of the iPod and the Apple Music Store to develop newer products such as the iPhone, which is the current cash cow of Apple.

Apple also offered seamless integration of the iPod with its other products such as the Mac PC, MacBook, Apple TV, iCloud, etc. to enhance the user experience for iPod users.

You as a marketer need to note that this is a common strategy in the maturity stage of the product life cycle where in you prolong the maturity stage. Or, in other words, delay the decline stage.

The beginning of the maturity stage can be indicated by Apple's competitors exiting the market due to their inability to implement any of the generic strategies devised by Michael Porter.

Decline Stage

Apple iPod's sales declined to a mere 26 million units in 2013 after reaching its peak sales of over 54 million units in 2008. Apple could not revive the iPod in spite of the introduction of the iPod Nano and iPod touch.

However, this was not a surprise for Apple as Steve Jobs had referred to the iPhone as the best iPod ever built during its launch in 2008.

The success of the iPhone cannibalized the sales of the iPod as the iPhone had all the functionalities of an iPod. It did not make sense for consumers to carry two different devices, i.e. a mobile phone and an MP3 when the Apple iPhone doubled up as a multi-purpose device.

The decline stage of the iPod can be characterized by deep discounts offered by Apple, which generally maintains a premium pricing strategy for most of its products.

It is likely these discounts played a role in the decline sales of the iPod as the iPod followed a different pricing strategy to Apple's iPhone and iPad.

Conclusion

The iPod is an excellent example of the fast-shortening product life cycle of products in the current age of fast technological development. While the iPod might have lost its credibility as a product, it was listed as one of the best inventions of the 21st Century, and the existing ecosystem of the iPod allowed the development of the iPhone and iPad, the present cash cow of Apple.   (917 words)

Writing: On the basis of the above case of iPod's PLC, write a brief introduction to the iPhone's PLC. You can search online or any other source to find out the details about the development of iPhone across history, and summarize it into a mini case by adopting the framework of PLC.

Word limit: 500 words.

Unit 10

Branding

🔔 Quote of the Unit:

"Brand is just a perception, and perception will match reality over time."

—Elon Musk

🔔 Learning Objectives:

1. Understand the definition and basic elements of a brand.
2. Understand the importance of branding.
3. Use both the knowledge and language learned in this unit to discuss and present issues related to brand and branding.

🔔 Pre-class Questions:

1. Why does company need a brand?
2. What is the benefit of owning a well-recognized brand?
3. When someone mentions a famous brand you are quite familiar with, what can you think of? Its symbol? Its design? Or something else?

Text A: Lead-in

Brand and Branding

Learning Resources

Branding is a strategy that is used by marketers to **differentiate** products and companies, and to build economic value for both the consumer and the brand owner.

- A brand is an identity that includes all sorts of components depending on the brand, e.g. Huawei **encapsulates** hi-tech, ethics, sustainability, etc.
- A brand is an image. The consumer perceives a brand as representing a particular **attribute**, e.g. Louis Vuitton represents luxury.
- A brand is a relationship where the consumer reflects upon him or herself through the experience of using a product or service.

Brand occupies space in the **perception** of the consumer, and is what results from the sum of what the consumer takes into consideration before making a purchase decision.

Therefore, branding is a strategy, and brand is what has meaning to the consumer.

There are some other terms used in branding:

Brand **equity** is the totality of the brand's attributes including reputation, symbols, **associations** and names.

The term "brand value" refers to a set of principles that a company wants to present to its customers.

There are a number of interpretations of the term brand:
- A brand is a logo. For example: McDonald's Golden Arches.
- A brand is a legal **instrument**, existing in a way similar to a patent or copyright.
- A brand is a company name, e.g., Coca-Cola.
- A brand is **shorthand** — not as straightforward. Here a brand that is perceived as having benefits in the mind of the consumer is recognized and acts as a shortcut to circumvent large chunks of information. So, when searching for a product or service in less familiar surroundings you will conduct an information search, but a recognized brand will help you reach a decision more conveniently.
- A brand is a risk reducer. The brand reassures you when you are in a new and unfamiliar **territory**.

- A brand is positioning. It is situated in relation to other brands in the mind of the consumer as better, worse, quicker, slower, etc.
- A brand is a personality, beyond functionality, e.g., Apple's iPod versus just any MP3 player.
- A brand is a cluster of values, e.g., Huawei is reliable, ethical, invaluable, innovative and so on.
- A brand is a vision. A brand vision is a brand's concept of its future. Where is the brand going? What does it want to achieve? What values does it want to stand for?
- A brand is added value, where the consumer sees value in a brand over and above its competition. For example: Audi over Volkswagen, and Volkswagen over Skoda — despite similarities.　(425 words)

Vocabulary and Useful Expressions

differentiate /ˌdɪfəˈrenʃieɪt/	v.	a quality or feature that differentiates one thing from another makes the two things different　使……差异化
encapsulate /ɪnˈkæpsəleɪt/	v.	(formal) to express the most important parts of sth. in a few words, a small space or a single object　简述, 概括, 压缩
attribute /əˈtrɪbjuːt/	n.	a quality or feature of sb./sth.　属性, 性质, 特征
perception /pəˈsepʃn/	n.	(formal) an idea, a belief or an image you have as a result of how you see or understand sth.　看法, 见解
equity /ˈekwətɪ/	n.	the value of a company's shares; the value of a property after all charges and debts have been paid　（公司的）股本, 资产净值
association /əˌsəʊsɪˈeɪʃn/	n.	an idea or a memory that is suggested by sb./sth.; a mental connection between ideas　联想, 联系
instrument /ˈɪnstrəmənt/	n.	(formal) something that is used by sb. in order to achieve sth.; a person or thing that makes sth. happen　促成某事的人（或事物), 手段
shorthand /ˈʃɔːthænd/	n.	a shorter way of saying or referring to sth., which may not be as accurate as the more complicated way of saying it (~ for sth.)　（对某事）简略的表达方式
territory /ˈterətrɪ/	n.	land that is under the control of a particular country or ruler　领土, 版图, 领地

Unit 10 Branding

Exercise 1. Language: Fill in the blanks with words or expressions from the above article.

1. It is highly recommended not to visit unexplored _____ single-handedly. You'd better form a team or find some skilled partners.
2. Trademark is a legal _____ that provides protection similar to that of patent or copyright.
3. It can _____ the brand personality, whether that is inspirational, trustworthy, or authoritative.
4. Your branding strategy should be able to build positive brand _____.
5. A brand is basically about a consumer's _____ of it, including the sum of a consumer's feelings, experiences, and thoughts about a product or service.
6. He has every _____ an excellent market should possess.
7. Marketers tend to add more features to their products in order to _____ from others.
8. A brand, especially a famous one, acts as a _____ to circumvent large chunks of information and make it easier for consumers to make a buying decision.
9. Brand, as a concept, has many _____, such as brand equity, brand personality, brand value, etc.
10. Brand _____ is the totality of the brand's attributes including reputation, symbols, associations and names.

Exercise 2. Knowledge: Answer the following questions briefly according to the above article.

1. What are the key objectives of a branding strategy?

2. What is the difference between a brand and branding?

3. Among the different aspects of a brand, such as the image, the values, the positioning, etc., which one do you think is the most fundamental?

4. What is a brand in essence according to your understanding?

Text B: Intensive Reading

Learning Resources

Branding and Major Branding Strategies

Branding

Branding is a marketing practice that helps individuals to distinguish and differentiate one company's products or services from others. Branding generally involves creating elements such as a name, logo, symbol, sign, mission statement, design and any other features that are **consistent** throughout multiple marketing communication activities and campaigns.

Branding helps build awareness and bring **credibility** to a company, creates customer loyalty as well as a number of other advantages. A product, service, person or place that is branded automatically gains the potential to develop a personality, recognition, and reputation among consumers.

In a word, your brand is a representation of who you are as a business, and using effective brand strategies can definitely help your business grow and reach beyond your target audience.

5 Types of Branding Strategies

A proper and effective branding strategy can be value-adding to your company depending on several factors such as target audience, industry, budget, and marketing campaigns. Here are 5 types of major branding strategies that are potentially able to help build brand equity for your business.

1. Product Branding

Product branding is one of the most popular branding types across history. Product branding focuses on making a single product **distinct** and **recognizable**. Symbols or designs are an essential part of product branding to help your customers identify your product easily.

For instance, Monster Energy® drinks have distinct

packaging and logos that make it easily distinguishable from Red Bull® energy drinks. Though the ingredients of such energy drinks may be similar to certain extent, the brand can possibly serve as a major element to appeal to consumers and **exert** influence on their choices.

2. Corporate Branding

Corporate branding is referring to the core value of a business and a philosophy that a business develops to present itself to the world and its own employees.

A company generally uses effective corporate brand to display the company's mission, personality, and core values in each point of contact it has with prospective customers, current customers, and past customers.

For example, Nike® has core values and mission statement that are recognizable across all of their platforms and products. Nike's mission statement says: "To bring inspiration and innovation to every athlete in the world." And its slogan, which can be found next to their famous *swoosh* check mark logo, goes as "JUST DO IT".

As a corporate brand, Nike positions itself as a brand for athletes, sports enthusiasts, and anyone who is passionate about fitness. They also make it clear that they believe anyone can be an athlete. (With a bit of careful thought, Nike added that every human that has a body can be regarded as an athlete.)

3. Service Branding

Unlike products, services do not even exist until they are purchased. Service branding, then, becomes doubly important. First, you must convince a prospect that the service is worth purchasing. Then, you must convince that current customer the service is worth using, sharing, and upgrading.

Service branding leverages the needs of the customer. Companies that use service branding seek to provide their customers with trustworthy service. They aim to use excellent customer service as a way to provide value to their customers.

Best Buy® is very successful in selling service agreements for a wide range of technology products with the Geek Squad. This is a good example of well-targeted and effective service branding that takes advantage of a retailer's **expertise** by launching a companion service brand.

4. Co-branding

Co-branding is a form of branding that connects different companies together. Essentially, co-branding is a marketing partnership between two or more businesses. This helps brands impact each other positively, and it may result in one growing its business, spreading brand awareness, and breaking into new markets.

For example, Frito Lay® and Taco Bell® came together and made the Doritos Locos Taco that appealed to audiences of both.

5. No-brand Branding

This type of branding is also known as **minimalist** branding. These brands are often **generic** brands that seek to let their products speak for themselves without all the **extras** many other companies provide their consumers with.

Some of the most **noteworthy** no-brand branding examples include Brandless® and m/f people®. As you can see on Brandless' website, their packaging, colors, and overall **aesthetic** is very simple. This aligns with their mission of providing fairly priced food to people without a typical brand. Despite the fact that Brandless® recently announced its closure, it is an excellent example of no-brand branding that saw great success for several years.

m/f people® adopts simplicity as its guiding principle in everything, from their branding and packaging to their product designs. For example, their skincare products are packaged in bottles with black and white colors and a simple font.

This decision to opt for simplicity aligns with their commitment to making gender-neutral products and pursuing their overall mission: "We aim to make life simple, so you can focus on what matters most." They don't need loud colors and flashy font. They want minimalist appeal. (833 words)

(**Source:** https://www.bluleadz.com/blog/types-of-branding-strategies.)

Vocabulary and Useful Expressions

branding /ˈbrændɪŋ/	n.	the activity of giving a particular name and image to goods and services so that people will be attracted to them and want to buy them 品牌建设，品牌推广
consistent /kənˈsɪstənt/	a.	always behaving in the same way, or having the same opinions, standards, etc. 一致的，始终如一的
credibility /ˌkredəˈbɪlətɪ/	n.	the quality that sb./sth. has that makes people believe or trust them 可信性，可靠性
distinct /dɪˈstɪŋkt/	a.	clearly different or of a different kind 截然不同的，有区别的
recognizable /ˌrekəgˈnaɪzəbl/	a.	easy to know or identify 容易认出的，易于识别的
exert /ɪgˈzɜːt/	v.	to use power or influence to affect sb./sth. 运用，行使，施加
expertise /ˌekspɜːˈtiːz/	n.	expert knowledge or skill in a particular subject, activity or job 专门知识，专门技能，专长
minimalist /ˈmɪnɪməlɪst/	n.	of, relating to, or done in the style of minimalism 极简主义的
generic /dʒəˈnerɪk/	a.	not using the name of the company that made it 无厂家商标的，无商标的
extras /ˈekstrəz/	n.	things which are not necessary in a situation, activity, or object, but which make it more comfortable, useful, or enjoyable 额外之物，附加物
noteworthy /ˈnəʊtwɜːðɪ/	a.	deserving to be noticed or to receive attention because it is unusual, important or interesting 值得注意的，显著的，重要的
aesthetic /iːsˈθetɪk/	n.	the aesthetic qualities and ideas of sth. 美感，审美观

Exercise 1. Language: Translate the following sentences into Chinese.

1. Branding is a marketing practice that helps individuals to distinguish and differentiate

one company's products or services from others.

2. Branding helps build awareness and bring credibility to a company, creates customer loyalty as well as a number of other advantages.

3. Your brand is a representation of who you are as a business, and using effective brand strategies can definitely help your business grow.

4. These brands are often generic brands that seek to let their products speak for themselves without all the extras many other companies provide their consumers with.

5. A company generally uses effective corporate brand to display the company's mission, personality, and core values.

6. This aligns with their mission of providing fairly priced food to people without a typical brand.

7. This decision to opt for simplicity aligns with their commitment to making gender-neutral products and pursuing their overall mission.

8. This is a good example of well-targeted and effective service branding that took advantage of a retailer's expertise by launching a companion service brand.

9. Though the ingredients of such energy drinks may be similar to certain extent, the brand can possibly serve as a major element to appeal to consumers and exert influence on their choices.

Exercise 2. Knowledge: True or false statements. If the following statements are true, write T; if false, write F.

1. Co-branding refers to the practice that two or more sub-brands of the same company cooperate to promote products. ( )
2. No-brand branding is often adopted by companies that adopt minimalism as their business philosophy. ( )
3. In service branding, it is necessary to convince the prospective customers that their services are tangible. ( )
4. Companies that adopt no-brand branding normally aims to reduce extras and provide fairly priced products to customers. ( )
5. Corporate branding generally promotes the company's corporate core values and philosophy as a whole to its target audience. ( )
6. Though Best Buy is a major retailer specializing in the sales of consumer electronics, it also excels in service branding. ( )
7. The core elements of a brand, once promoted through multiple ways, may vary in order to fit the different characteristics of channels and platforms. ( )
8. Product branding focuses on making a single product, instead of the corporate itself, distinct and recognizable. ( )
9. A brand can be regarded as a representation of the company as a whole. ( )
10. A proper branding strategy can help build consumer awareness and bring credibility for a company, creates customer loyalty. ( )

Exercise 3. Language: Fill in the blanks with words or expressions from the above article.

1. If a company adopts a branding strategy, it needs to keep its branding messages _____ across all channels of marketing.
2. Recommendations from two previous clients helped to establish her _____.
3. The problem is that most local authorities lack the _____ to deal sensibly in this market.
4. The new product design clearly reflects the _____ value that the product development appreciates.
5. The company's minimalist philosophy will surely _____ influence on the product team's decision making process.
6. As a company committed to providing fairly priced products to price-sensitive customers, they intend to reduce all the unnecessary _____ other producers put on their products.
7. It is quite _____ that though the two beverages are sold at almost the same

price, the ingredients the producers use are dramatically different.
8. Marketers should always bear in mind that it is necessary to _____ brand awareness to drive growth.
9. An effective branding strategy can build great brand image, and thus appeal to _____ customers, thus enlarge the company's customer base.
10. A brand with _____ features different from other brands may attract consumers' attention more easily.

Oral practice: Work with your partners. Share your findings of real-life examples that adopt one of the 5 branding strategies. Some key elements should be mentioned: the company's name, its specialization, its target customers, the branding strategy that it adopts, how effective it is. You can talk about either domestic or international brands. You are encouraged to use both the language and knowledge learned in this article. You should firstly do the research, write down key points and take turns to report. Then one student should report the findings orally to the whole class on behalf of the team.

Text C: Extensive Reading

Learning Resources

Brand Storytelling: 4 Inspiring Examples of Brand Story

By Anete Ezera

What Is Brand Storytelling?

Brand storytelling is the act of using emotion-evoking narrative techniques to establish a value-driven connection with your customers. Emotion-evoking narrative techniques include power words like crazy, imagine, love, and hate. Visuals like different images and data visualizations play an important role in painting the picture of your brand's story.

In short, a story humanizes your brand and makes it easier for your customers to connect with it. It applies that emotional connection to your products or services, making it a memorable experience rather than a simple exchange of goods. Most importantly, it centers your customers as protagonists in your story and allows them to participate in the narrative.

What Defines a Great Brand Story?

Many factors play a crucial role in a brand's story. A great story consists of eye-catching visuals, compelling narratives, a hero figure, and others.

Conflict

What makes stories so compelling? A conflict that needs to be resolved or overcome. A story without a conflict or problem isn't going to capture people's attention. However, companies usually don't want to share a problem they've dealt with. Most would rather convey a flawless image of themselves that's so perfect at times it almost appears to be disingenuous. It's easy to sugarcoat everything, but if you want to connect with your audience, your brand should shed the perfectionist image.

People don't relate to perfectionism or infinite success. They relate to emotional journeys with ups and downs. People value transparency, especially from companies. Therefore, be confident in your truth and share the adversities you've overcome. Inspire your audience with a positive approach to a problem or conflict, and share the lessons you've learned. This way, your brand will become more trustworthy for your customers, and you'll be able to create a more meaningful relationship with your audience.

Consistency and Transparency

Once you've shared your brand's story, there's no going back. You can't change your story or act in a certain way that goes against the values and beliefs that you've shared. You have to stay consistent with your storytelling and make sure that your actions correspond to the brand story you're trying to tell.

If your audience starts to recognize some inconsistencies, you risk losing credibility. That's why it's crucial to have your brand's story reflect your values as truthfully as possible.

Visuals

The way you communicate your brand's story is crucial. When promoting your brand through social media, your website, and other channels, the first thing your audience notices is visual.

Your visual content will ultimately carry the message for you. Ensure that whatever way you convey your brand's story, your visual content can support it the whole way through. Also, visuals need to highlight the most important aspects of your narrative.

Brand Story Examples

Now that we have listed three key ingredients to an effective brand story, let's look at some successful brand story examples for inspiration.

Google's Year in Search

Google has always been on top of its branding. The story-centered campaigns have spoken to millions of people and strengthened their brand. A recent high was Google's Year in Search video, which included the most searched words and phrases of 2021. The data-driven story consisted of emotion-evoking video clips that revealed the highs and lows of 2021. (Input "Google — Year in Search" in your search engine and you'll find out.)

Portraying human emotions in a video is a powerful way to tug at one's heartstrings. It's natural for people to mimic and respond to other people's emotions. As a result, people feel more connected to others and the story. This video is a perfect example of how important visual content is in storytelling. Also, notice how this story isn't sugarcoated but includes conflict by sharing the low points people experienced in 2021.

The Body Shop

The cosmetics, skincare, and perfume company was the first in the beauty industry to prioritize fair trade. They're also widely recognized as cruelty-free, meaning that animals aren't used to test their products. The Body Shop's strong values have always appeared in advertising. When people think about cruelty-free and fair trade cosmetics, the Body Shop is at the top of their minds.

Founded in 1976, the company has successfully made its place in the beauty industry and continues attracting new customers. What's their secret, you ask? Staying consistent and placing its values and people at the forefront of its brand story has helped them strengthen their place in the market and gain trustworthy customers. On social media, they not only communicate their values but also take their followers on a journey to meet different communities that supply the product ingredients. As a result, their brand story consists of several stories from communities all over the world.

Spotify Wrapped

Last December, were you curious to see your Spotify Wrapped? Did you share it on your social media? Many of us did. More than 90 million people engaged with Spotify Wrapped in 2020, making it a huge success.

Spotify Wrapped summarizes a listener's streaming history for the last year. The summary includes top songs, albums, genres, podcasts, and more. All that is presented in a neatly organized way with engaging visuals, audio clips from songs, and data visualizations, making it a compelling story to watch.

The data-driven narrative was highly successful because the story wasn't about Spotify. Instead, it was about its customers. The personalized streaming history placed Spotify listeners at the forefront of the brand's identity. As a result, the company strengthened its brand and its relationship with its customers and improved its user experience.

Making your customers the protagonists of your brand's story is a great way to build a strong community and increase engagement. You want your customers to be your advocates. Letting them be the star of the show will motivate them to stay loyal to your brand.

Nike

"Emotional ties builds long-term relationships with the consumer, and that's what our campaigns are about," states Phil Knight confidently, the co-founder and chairman emeritus of Nike, Inc., in *Harvard Business Review*.

Nike is one of the most influential storytellers in the sports industry. And the key to their brand storytelling success has been emotion-evoking narratives that athletes can relate to. They directly speak to their audience, showcasing a range of emotions like excitement, determination, competitiveness, and others that people experience in sports.

In one of its most successful advertisements, you can see sports legends like Michael Jordan and John McEnroe next to amateur athletes, competing and having fun. This ad perfectly plays into Nike's brand story about the fitness community and that anyone can achieve amazing things with determination and the right shoes.

Brand storytelling can help you strengthen your place in the market, expand and reach your target audience, and make your products more appealing. With the right concept and tools like captivating data visualizations, social media posts, and videos, you can capitalize on brand storytelling to make it a success.   (1161 words)

(**Source:** https://infogram.com/blog/brand-storytelling-brand-story-examples/.)

 Task

Writing: Find an appealing brand story (either written or presented in visual form) of a famous Chinese brand online or from other sources. Write a brief introduction to it and reveal why you think the brand story is appealing and successful. You are suggested to seek for examples from famous Chinese brands such as Huawei, Xiaomi, Nio, DJI, etc.

Word limit: 300 words.

Unit 11

Market Segmentation

🔔 Quote of the Unit:

"Market segmentation is a natural result of the vast differences among people."

—Donald A. Norman

🔔 Learning Objectives:

1. Understand the definition of market segment and market segmentation.
2. Understand the different criteria applied to market segmentation.
3. Master words and expressions used to discuss issues related to market segmentation.
4. Use both the language and knowledge learned in this unit to discuss topics related to market segmentation.

🔔 Pre-class Questions:

1. What do we call the practice of grouping consumers according to their shared characteristics?
2. Is it necessary to identify different groups of consumers?
3. What standards or criteria can be applied when it comes to grouping consumers?

Text A: Lead-in

Learning Resources

Successful Segmentation-based Cases

Adapted from Rob Petersen

Segmentation is the process of defining and subdividing a large **homogeneous** market into clearly **identifiable** segments having similar needs, wants, or demand characteristics. The importance of segmentation is that it allows a business to precisely reach a consumer with specific needs and wants. This enables the company to use resources more effectively, make better strategic marketing decisions and realize new **revenue** streams.

Here are 3 segmentation case studies that opened up new revenues for brands.

Case 1: E-commerce retailer BustedTees has a global customer base. It used to send all of its e-mails at the same time of day. The company segmented its e-mail list by time zone then set its campaigns to be delivered at 10 am local time. BustedTees added an extra layer of segmentation using past data on individual open times to develop a personalized send time for each **subscriber**. The results were:

- 8% lift in e-mail revenue overnight from personalized send time.
- 17% increase in total e-mail response rate.
- 11% higher clickthrough rate.
- 7.6% increase in post-click site engagement.

Case 2: The quick rise of Smartphone cameras was **eclipsing** the development of the digital camera market. The kids segment was an underdeveloped market. Canon was trying to extend its target segment from parents-to-be to parents with kids, targeting mainly 5–9 years old and their parents. **Dubbed** Kidictionary, a three months contest asked participants to **interoperate** an ordinary word in a creative way through photography, and then to share online and social media. In order to drive better engagement, the company planted the seed via key opinion bloggers and online advertising to draw eyeballs. The campaign website pulled in 3,559 (64.3%) new visitors and 1,976 (35.7%) returning visitors. In total, the site recorded 5,535 visitors per month and over 180 visitors per day. Total submission on the "Kidictionary" reached 344 and 348 users. The campaign gained 40% market share on low-end DC compared to last year.

Case 3: By carefully targeting its intended audiences and using the social media platforms where these consumers actively participate, the Lego Group was able to effectively reach its customers and offer them the kind of online experience. The company used six distinct **personas** to categorize their customers based on purchase and usage rates. These six personas ranged from consumers who were highly involved with the Lego Group's products, such as those who helped shape product design to those having no experience with the brand. By actively engaging these people and giving them special attention, the Lego Group stood the best chance of encouraging them to be the company's most **ardent advocates**. The Lego Group became the world's fourth largest toy manufacturer, capturing approximately 6.9% of the global market share of toy sales and continues to sustain a high growth rate, as well as showing a net profit of about $688 million dollars for the year. (477 words)

Vocabulary and Useful Expressions

homogeneous /ˌhɒməˈdʒiːniəs/	a.	consisting of things or people that are all the same or all of the same type 由相同（或同类型）事物（或人）组成的，同种类的，同质化的
identifiable /aɪˌdentɪˈfaɪəbl/	a.	that can be recognized 可识别的，可辨认的
revenue /ˈrevənjuː/	n.	money that a company, organization, or government receives from people （公司、组织的）收入，收益，（政府的）财政收入，税收
subscriber /səbˈskraɪbə(r)/	n.	a person who pays to receive a service 消费者，用户
eclipse /ɪˈklɪps/	v.	to make sb./sth. seem dull or unimportant by comparison 使失色，使相形见绌，使丧失重要性
dub /dʌb/	v.	to give sb./sth. a particular name, often in a humorous or critical way 把……戏称为，给……起绰号
interoperate /ˌɪntəˈɒpəreɪt/	v.	to operate together 交互操作
persona /pəˈsəʊnə/	n.	the aspect of their character or nature that they present to other people 表象人格
ardent /ˈɑːdnt/	a.	very enthusiastic and showing strong feelings about sth./sb. 热烈的，激情的
advocate /ˈædvəkeɪt/	n.	a person who supports or speaks in favour of sb. or of a public plan or action 拥护者，支持者，提倡者

Unit 11 Market Segmentation

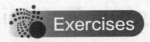

Exercise 1. Language: Fill in the blanks with words or expressions from the above article.

1. The quick rise of new energy cars will definitely _____ the development of traditional cars.
2. He's been one of the most _____ supporters of the administration's policy.
3. The new App has witnessed a very rapid growth last month, with the number of _____ soaring to 1 million.
4. Currently the market is saturated with _____ products that are similar in every aspect.
5. As an _____ of the new marketing practice, the company has already manifested its success to the world.
6. The gap in the market is easily _____ business opportunity for some.
7. A source revealed that the high tech company was planning to _____ its new robot as "Iron Egg".
8. The company used 9 distinct _____ to categorize their users based on frequency of purchase and usage rates.

Exercise 2. Knowledge: Answer the following questions briefly according to the above article.

1. What adjustments did BustedTees do to improve its business?
   _____
   _____

2. What factor eclipsed the business development of Canon?
   _____
   _____

3. What campaign did it take to extend its customer base?
   _____
   _____

4. What did Lego do to improve its customers' experience?
   _____
   _____

Text B: Intensive Reading

On Market Segmentation

Market segmentation is a very fundamental process a marketer should **undergo** before making further marketing decisions concerning target audience, new product development, etc. It is so important that it deserves a detailed introduction.

Let's firstly have a look at this word: SEGMENTATION. According to the Collins Dictionary, segmentation is the dividing of something into parts, which are loosely connected.

Given our knowledge of **lexicology**, especially word formation, we may guess that the word segmentation comes from the word segment. Yes, this guessing is absolutely correct. Segment can be used either as a noun or a verb. When it is used as a noun, it is pronounced like segment ['segment], with the accent at the very beginning of the word. A segment of something is one part of it considered separately from the rest. Therefore, a market segment is one part of the market.

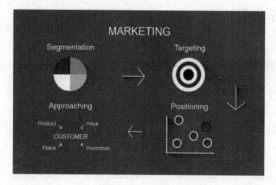

When it is used as a verb, if you prefer the British way, it is pronounced like segment /seg'ment/, with the accent at the latter syllable of the word. By its original meaning, to segment /seg'ment/ means to divide something into different parts.

So, if a company segments a market, it divides it into separate parts, usually in order to more precisely identify the target consumers and improve its market positioning and explore more marketing opportunities.

Now we can see that market segmentation means the act of dividing the market into different parts. But why do marketers need to do so?

The primary reason is: there is not a single company that is capable enough (with all kinds of resources) to develop a product that can satisfy all the consumers in this world. It needs to focus on a specific group of consumers which share similar needs and characteristics and then develop a product or several products to satisfy their needs.

Unit 11 Market Segmentation

The second reason is that people are different in their backgrounds, education, needs, tastes and preferences. So, they need and prefer different types of products. Then those consumers with similar needs, behaviors and preferences can be grouped together to from different smaller segments. Hence, it will provide more **attainable** and realistic opportunities for those companies.

Different companies adopt different approaches to market segmentation. But generally, there are several common criteria. For instance, marketers may use **demography** to segment the market. The word demography refers to the study of human populations, including their size, growth, **density**, and distribution, and **statistics** regarding birth, marriage, disease and death. This is a very important factor and helps to divide the population into market segments and target markets.

A typical example of demography is classifying groups of people according to the year they were born. These classifications can be referred to as baby boomers who were born between 1946 and 1964, shortly after the end of the World War Two; Generation X, who were born between 1965 and 1976; and Generation Y, who were born between 1977 and 1994. In China people may divide the population according to the decade that they were born and label them as post-80s and post-90s.

Each classification has different characteristics. This can be beneficial to marketers as they can decide who their products would benefit most and tailor their marketing plans to attract that segment.

Besides, there are other ways of dividing the market into different smaller groups.

For instance, group people according to the region, country or even climate of the places where they live. They can also be grouped according to their psychographic features like lifestyle, personality, values and attitudes to life. Customers can still be grouped on the basis of their actual behaviors towards products and services.

In order to better identify and segment the customers, people develop more comprehensive ways to do the market segmentation.

In the UK, they have the so-called ACORN model, which stands for A Classification of Residential Neighborhoods.

ACORN is a powerful consumer classification model that segments the UK population. By analyzing demographic data, social factors, population and consumer behavior, it provides precise information and an understanding of different types of people.

ACORN segments postcodes and neighborhoods in the UK into 6 categories, 18 groups and 62 types, three of which are not private households. By analyzing significant social factors and population behavior, it provides precise information and in-depth understanding of the different types of people who live in a particular area. With this information you can learn more about your customers' behavior and identify prospects who most resemble your target customers, define local demand for products and services and understand what drives effective customer communication strategies.

In the US they use a model called ABC Socio-economic Categories which uses people's income level, professions and social status to group them. By using these criteria people are grouped into more specific and distinct groups that are different from others.

Table 11.1 ABC socio-economic categories

Social Grade	Social Status	Occupation of Head of Household or Chief Income Earner
A	upper middle class	higher managerial, administrative or professional
B	middle class	intermediate managerial, administrative or professional
C1	lower middle class	junior managerial, administrative or professional; clerical
C2	**skilled** working class	skilled manual workers
D	working class	semi-skilled and unskilled manual workers
E	those at lowest level of **subsistence**	state pensioners or widows (no other earner); casual or lowest grade workers

Note: The head of household is usually the person in the household with the highest income.

Marketers also use the data to build up a customer **profile**, which is a brief image of a typical consumer. For example, a group of educated men in their 40s with monthly income higher than 4,000 pounds, who love their families and sports and are willing to spend money on keeping fit.

In a word, market segmentation is one very fundamental and essential step in market analysis. Its importance lies in the fact that only after market segmentation process can companies find their target markets and develop more suitable and satisfactory products to cater to target customers' needs.　(998 words)

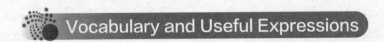

Vocabulary and Useful Expressions

undergo /ˌʌndəˈgəʊ/	v.	to experience sth., especially a change or sth. unpleasant　经历，经受（变化、不快的事等）
lexicology /ˌleksɪˈkɒlədʒɪ/	n.	the study of the form, meaning and behaviour of words　词汇学
attainable /əˈteɪnəbl/	a.	that you can achieve　可达到的，可获得的
demography /dɪˈmɒgrəfɪ/	n.	the changing number of births, deaths, diseases, etc. in a community over a period of time; the scientific study of these changes　人口统计，人口统计学
density /ˈdensətɪ/	n.	the quality of being dense; the degree to which sth. is dense　密集，稠密
statistics /stəˈtɪstɪks/	n.	a collection of information shown in numbers　统计数字，统计资料
skilled /skɪld/	a.	having enough ability, experience and knowledge to be able to do sth. well　有技能的，熟练的
subsistence /səbˈsɪstəns/	n.	the state of having just enough money or food to stay alive　勉强维持生活
profile /ˈprəʊfaɪl/	n.	a description of sb./sth. that gives useful information　概述，简介，传略

Exercises

Exercise 1. Language: Translate the following sentences into Chinese.

1. Market segmentation is a very fundamental process a marketer should undergo before

making further marketing decisions.

2. So, if a company segments a market, it divides it into separate parts, usually in order to more precisely identify the target consumers.

3. Marketers also use the data to build up a customer profile, which is a brief image of a typical consumer.

4. By analyzing demographic data, social factors, population and consumer behaviour, it provides precise information and an understanding of different types of people.

5. In order to better identify and segment the customers, people develop more comprehensive ways to do the market segmentation.

6. In a word, market segmentation is one very fundamental and essential step in market analysis.

7. They can also be grouped according to their psychographic features like lifestyle, personality, values and attitudes to life.

8. The word demography refers to the study of human populations, including their size, growth, density, and distribution, and statistics regarding birth, marriage, disease and death.

9. Then those consumers with similar needs, behaviors and preferences can be grouped together to from different smaller segments.

10. In China people may divide the population according to the decade that they were born

Unit 11 Market Segmentation

and label them as post-80s and post-90s.

_____

_____

Exercise 2. Knowledge: True or false statements. If the following statements are true, write T; if false, write F.

1. Market segmentation is a fundamental process which has to be done before selecting the target customers. (   )
2. Consumer demographic data include their lifestyles, attitudes and opinions towards certain things. (   )
3. Consumer psychographic data can be very important in helping draw a customer profile. (   )
4. The year of birth can be used as one of the psychographic criteria to group customers. (   )
5. The ACORN model mainly deals with people's geographic and demographic data combined. (   )
6. It is also reasonable if marketers group people according to the climate situation of the places where they live. (   )
7. The ABC Socio-economic Categories mainly adopts economic situation and occupation as well as social class to group people. (   )
8. It is possible that a giant company, given enormous resources of all kinds, can develop and promote a product to satisfy the needs of human beings around the world. (   )
9. The term Generation X is used to refer to people born between 1946 and 1964, shortly after the end of the World War Two. (   )
10. A customer profile normally include demographic and psychographic information of a typical customer of one business. It is also the description of the general characteristics of its target customers. (   )

Exercise 3. Knowledge: Answer the following questions briefly according to the above article.

1. What should be done before selecting a target market?

_____

_____

2. What criteria can be adopted in the market segmentation process?

_____

_____

167

3. What are the possible outcomes of market segmentation?

4. Which criteria do you think would be more suitable to segment the market when it comes to defining the target customers of a smartphone?

5. Can you find out any flaw in the ABC socio-economic categories?

6. What are the possible benefits of adopting ACORN as a segmentation tool?

Oral practice: Work with your partners. Select one product of a famous brand. Do some research and find out the main characteristics of its target customer. Exchange ideas with your partners and try to describe the general customer profile of it. You can refer to the article for an example of customer profile description.

Then one student, on behalf of your team, should report your findings orally to the whole class.

Text C: Extensive Reading

Learning Resources

Market Segmentation Example for Car Insurance

Insurance is an intangible service to consumers, where they essentially buy it for security and peace of mind. Insurance protects them against unexpected damage of their motor vehicle and consequential financial loss. It is not a product that consumers actively seek out — they just know that they should have it, and in some jurisdictions certain types of car insurance are mandatory.

Insurance is one of those products where the majority of consumers are less involved in the purchase decision (primarily due to lack of interest) and, as a result, consumer typically sees very little differentiation between competitive offers. This will mean that price and brand and distribution channel will play a more important role in the successful sale of insurance products, as opposed to the quality and design of the product itself.

In this example of market segmentation for car insurance, six different market segments have been identified, which include:
- Fully covered;
- Highly loyal;
- Price shoppers;
- Make it easy;
- Just the basics;
- Pick and choose.

Fully Covered

This market segment of consumers is highly risk-averse and tends to be "heavy users" of insurance. They will tend to ensure all their assets, such as house and car, as well as take out life insurance and income insurance. This gives them tremendous peace of mind and financial security.

They tend to be, but not always, higher income earners who see themselves as financially savvy, and do not understand why some people do not have insurance.

They are more involved in the purchase decision than the other market segments and tend to review the product details and compare products on that basis. Price is not a major consideration in their purchase decision and they will generally take out large amounts of insurance cover.

Highly Loyal

This market segment is also quite risk-averse, but do not have the extent or the volume of insurance that the fully covered segment has. Instead, they view brand loyalty (that is, being a long-term customer of one insurance company) as something that gives them more security and benefits. They believe that their future insurance claims are more likely to be paid if they have a significant history with the insurance company.

This segment becomes the core customer base for higher branded insurance companies, as these customers are also attracted to well-known and reputable insurance firms.

As a result, they are highly unlikely to switch, and are quite price insensitive. A strong brand and a long-term relationship are the key benefits of they seek in the insurance market.

Price Shoppers

Price shoppers perceive very little difference between competitive offerings of insurance and will make their decision on a price basis. They see no benefit in loyalty and have the perception that insurance companies are more generous to new customers than to existing customers.

It is not uncommon for this segment of consumers to shop around every year for insurance and even switch back and forth between insurance companies over time.

Make It Easy

These are convenience motivated consumers. They know they need insurance, but see it as a hassle to fill out forms and paperwork. They are attracted by offers of quick and easy insurance or may deal through a third party agent. They are quite likely to have all their insurance with the firm.

They are not concerned with price or the product details, or even who their insurance is with. Perhaps not surprisingly, this market segment is generally quite profitable (once they have been acquired by an insurance firm), as they are very loyal, price insensitive, and less likely to make an insurance claim.

Just the Basics

This market segment of consumers has a perception that you just need basic cover. They see themselves as smart shoppers and not needing to pay for "fancy" extra pieces of cover that they will probably never use.

In many ways, they are like the consumer in a supermarket, who sees themselves as a "smart shopper" and generally gets a better deal than other people. Therefore, they are not necessarily price shoppers, but will make decisions more a rational price-value basis.

Pick and Choose

This first market segment within the car insurance market is attracted to insurance products that offer flexibility and the ability to add and subtract components of the insurance cover. They have a good understanding of their insurance needs and are reasonably involved in the purchase decision.

They differ from just the basics market segment in that they will seek out specific levels of additional coverage for their particular situation. They expect some form of discount for not being fully covered, so price is somewhat important to them.　　(776 words)

(**Source:** https://www.segmentationstudyguide.com/understanding-market-segmentation/market-segmentation-examples/market-segmentation-example-motor-vehicle-insurance/.)

Writing: Choose an industry or a type of product. Try to group its customers into three segments according to certain criteria. You can choose from cars, banking, insurance, cosmetics, smartphone, charities, beverage, fitness center, etc. Write down the general situation of the type of product or industry, and describe briefly the three segments. The above article is for your reference in terms of content and format.

Word limit: 300 words.

Unit 12

Customer Needs

Customer Needs

🔔 *Quote of the Unit:*

"Sell the problem you solve. Not the product you make."

—Unknown

🔔 *Learning Objectives:*

1. Understand the definition of customer needs.
2. Understand the major differences between needs and wants.
3. Understand the major structure of Maslow's Hierarchy of Needs and the meaning of different categories.
4. Master the key words and terms used in discussing customer needs.
5. Apply both the knowledge and language learned in this unit to analyze cases related to customer needs.

🔔 *Pre-class Questions:*

1. What kinds of needs do human beings normally have?
2. Have you ever tried to classify our needs into different categories according to certain criteria?
3. According to your own experience, which type of need is the most difficult to meet?

Unit 12 Customer Needs

Text A: Lead-in

Learning Resources

Mr. Johnson, a senior marketer for a **high street** bank named Wells Fargo, delivered a lecture to the financial management **trainees** about how to promote their products according to Maslow's **Hierarchy** of Needs:

"Just imagine that Mr. Black, a senior **professional**, one of our high-value clients comes to see us and discuss about the **pension** plan for his retirement. Of course, we talk out his basic needs, hopes and dreams for his retirement life.

To start with, we normally talk about his concerns for meeting his **physiological** needs; by this we mean how he will be able to pay for his food and drink, electricity and gas bills to sustain his basic living needs. This is often the major customer concern, simply because human beings need to survive in this society first.

Then we will go to his safety needs: how our client can protect himself and his family after retirement. Normally he will need to invest more in life insurance to help him gain greater sense of safety.

After that, we think about his social needs. Will he still be able to afford the golf club membership which is rather expensive? This is also a must-consider factor since he still has to socialize with his friends and relatives. As the old saying goes, no man is an island. We are social animals, and we have the need to feel being connected with others.

Later, we go to his **esteem** needs. As he is a successful professional working in a high-income industry, he currently has the ability to own and drive a Porsche Cayenne to work and **unwind**. So will he still be able to afford a Porsche concerns his esteem need: to maintain his current life-style and social status.

At last we go to talk about his **self-actualization** needs. When we mention the term self-actualization, we mean his personal projects and dreams. We need to help him figure out how much money he needs to invest in which pension plan so that he will be able to travel around the world with his wife when he retires from work.

Ok, finally let me sum up: there are different types of needs among human beings. From the bottom to top are physiological needs, safety needs, social needs, esteem needs and self-actualization needs. Altogether they make Malsow's Hierarchy of Needs.

The most important thing we have to remember is, each type of need represents different types of products that are made and marketed to meet people's needs. Therefore, understanding customer needs can be very essential to developing and marketing products.

Now let me ask you some questions..." (439 words)

Useful Words and Expressions

high street		the main street of a town, where most shops/stores, banks, etc. are 大街（城镇的主要商业街道）
trainee /ˌtreɪˈniː/	n.	a person who is being taught how to do a particular job 接受培训者，实习生
hierarchy /ˈhaɪərɑːki/	n.	a system that ideas or beliefs can be arranged into 层次体系
professional /prəˈfeʃnl/	n.	a person who does a job that needs special training and a high level of education 专门人员，专业人士，专家
pension /ˈpenʃn/	n.	an amount of money paid regularly by a government or company to sb. who is considered to be too old or too ill/sick to work 养老金，退休金，抚恤金
physiological /ˌfɪziəˈlɒdʒɪk(ə)l/	a.	of or relating to the biological study of physiology 生理学的，生理的
esteem /ɪˈstiːm/	n.	(formal) great respect and admiration; a good opinion of sb. 尊重，敬重，好评
unwind /ˌʌnˈwaɪnd/	v.	to stop worrying or thinking about problems and start to relax 放松，轻松
self-actualization /ˌself ˌæktʃuəlaɪˈzeɪʃən/	n.	the process of establishing oneself as a whole person, able to develop one's abilities and to understand oneself 自我实现

Unit 12 Customer Needs

Exercise 1. Language: Fill in the blanks with words or expressions from the above article.

1. The company has recently hired some financial management _____ to supplement its staff turnover.
2. Though we are still two decades away from our retirement, we have to seriously consider our _____ plan.
3. We work so hard but only earn a meager salary just enough to _____ our basic living.
4. People often buy expensive things to meet their self _____ needs.
5. Although the economy is currently experiencing a recession, some _____ _____ banks are still expanding their businesses.
6. Human beings need to know how to _____ so that they can recover from a hard day's work.
7. Transforming a new graduate from an amateur to a _____ takes time, education and practice.
8. The _____ of Needs proposed by Abraham Maslow is well adopted across disciplines including socio-psychology, human resource management, marketing, economics.
9. The need for self _____ is the most difficult to achieve among all other categories of needs.
10. _____ needs refer to those basic needs that human beings have to meet first so that they can survive.

Exercise 2. Knowledge: Answer the following questions briefly according to the above article.

1. Can you sum up what are the five categories of needs according to the lecture?
   _____
   _____

2. Can you find out other names for the five types of needs mentioned in the lecture? For example, self-actualization is also called self-fulfillment.
   _____
   _____

3. What is the significance of identifying and understanding customers' needs?
   _____
   _____

177

Text B: Intensive Reading

Customer Needs

Learning Resources

"Customer needs" is a very interesting and **inspiring** topic. It has attracted the attention of many marketers and researchers, simply because satisfying customer needs is the ultimate purpose of developing new products and marketing.

If we want to probe into customer needs we need to have a look at a very famous theory in social psychology: Abraham Maslow's Hierarchy of Needs.

Maslow's Hierarchy of Needs is often **portrayed** in the shape of a pyramid with the most fundamental needs at the bottom, and the need for self-actualization at the top, as shown in Figure 12.1.

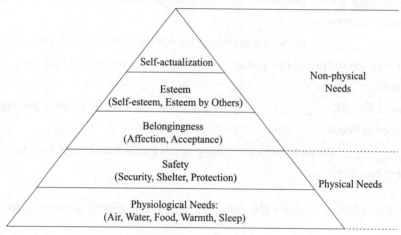

Figure 12.1 Maslow's Hierarchy of Need

The most fundamental and basic four layers of the pyramid contain what Maslow called "**deficiency** needs": esteem, friendship and love, security, and physiological needs. If these "deficiency needs" are not met, the individual will feel anxious and **tense**.

Maslow's theory suggests that the most basic level of needs must be met before the individual will strongly desire (or focus motivation upon) the secondary or higher-level needs. However, the human brain is a complex system and has **parallel** processes running at the same time, thus many different motivations from various levels of Maslow's hierarchy can occur at the same time.

Instead of stating that the individual focuses on a certain need at any given time, Maslow claimed that a certain need "dominates" the human organism. Physiological needs such as water, food are the physical requirements for human survival. Clothing and **shelter** provide necessary protection. If these requirements are not met, the human body cannot **function** properly and will ultimately **cease** to exist.

Physiological needs are thought to be the most important: they should be met first. Once a person's physiological needs are relatively satisfied, their safety needs take **precedence** and dominate behaviors. People may demand physical safety, financial security, job security, savings accounts, insurance policies, disability accommodations, etc.

After physiological and safety needs are fulfilled, the third level of human needs is **interpersonal** and involves feelings of belongingness. According to Maslow, humans need to feel a sense of belonging and acceptance among their social groups, regardless of whether these groups are large or small. They need to communicate and establish their interpersonal relationships with people around them. This need for the sense of belonging may overcome the physiological and security needs depending on the strength of the peer pressure.

All humans have a need to feel respected. This includes the need to have self-esteem and self-respect. Esteem presents the typical human desire to be accepted and valued by others.

People often engage in a profession or hobby to gain recognition and respect. These activities give the person a sense of contribution or value. People with low self-esteem often crave for respect from others and more interested in seeking fame or glory.

"What a man can be, he must be." This quotation forms the basis of the perceived need for self-actualization. This level of need refers to what a person's full potential is and the realization of that potential. Maslow describes this level as the desire to accomplish everything that one can to become the most that one can be. Individuals may perceive or focus on this need very specifically.

For example, one individual may have the strong desire to become an ideal parent. For another, the desire may be expressed athletically, like **surpassing** the previous PB (personal best achievements). For some people, climbing the highest mountain in the world is regarded as one way of achieving self-actualization. For others, it may be expressed in painting, pictures, or inventions. Maslow believed that to understand this level of need the person must not only achieve the previous needs but master them.

Now let's sum up the hierarchy a little bit: it consists of five levels of needs; from the very bottom to the top of the pyramid are the physiological needs, safety needs, belonging needs, esteem needs and self-actualization needs. Needs of different levels may occur at the same time, but some needs may dominate the human organism at a certain period of time.

For example, when a person is very hungry, his need for food will **suppress** his other needs. Another example is when a person persists in having greater achievement in certain fields, his other needs will not be as obvious as this need.

The fact that human beings have different needs provides great opportunities for many different types of companies. It is said that the success of every company is dependent on its ability to create products and services that address **unmet** customer needs.

The simplest example is, there are many companies that supply food and drink for satisfying the need for physical survival. Many clothing companies supply clothes to cover and protect human bodies. There are also many real estate developers to supply houses and apartments, to satisfy people's need for shelter. In order to satisfy people's safety needs, many insurance companies provide insurance **policies** to help protect people against future loss of health or wealth. Many **pharmaceutical** manufacturers supply medicines to help people fight against diseases and illnesses in order to maintain physical safety and well-being.

In order to satisfy people's need for a sense of belonging, many clubs and institutes help people socialize. Online socializing apps like WeChat, Line and WhatsApp are developed to help people communicate and socialize more conveniently and effectively.

In order to help satisfy people need for esteem and respect, many companies develop products of higher quality and of course, higher price.

For example, luxury car makers launch new editions of Porsche, Ferrari and Lamborghini to help people manifest their social status and win respect and admiration from others. In the case of satisfying self-actualization needs, do you still remember I've just mentioned that some people realize this by climbing the highest mountain of the world? In fact, it is very difficult for an ordinary, untrained person to achieve this. Therefore, companies that provide this kind of training and equipment come into being and help them realize this dream.

In a word, marketers should be very clear about people's basic needs and their changing needs. Only by carefully observing these needs can marketers spot any future business opportunities.

Please remember, the development of every product or service should be based on real customer needs. Never develop any product that can be only seen as an answer to a non-existent problem. Otherwise, no one will buy the product, and the business may flop and fail. (1100 words)

Useful Words and Expressions

inspiring /ɪnˈspaɪərɪŋ/	*a.*	exciting and encouraging you to do or feel sth. 鼓舞人心的，激励的，启发灵感的
portray /pɔːˈtreɪ/	*v.*	to show sb./sth. in a picture; to describe sb./sth. in a piece of writing 描绘，描画，描写
deficiency /dɪˈfɪʃnsi/	*n.*	the state of not having, or not having enough of, sth. that is essential 缺乏，缺少，不足
tense /tens/	*a.*	nervous or worried, and unable to relax 神经紧张的，担心的，不能松弛的
parallel /ˈpærəlel/	*a.*	very similar or taking place at the same time 极相似的，同时发生的
shelter /ˈʃeltə(r)/	*n.*	the fact of having a place to live or stay, considered as a basic human need 居所，住处
function /ˈfʌŋkʃn/	*v.*	to work in the correct way 起作用，正常工作，运转
cease /siːs/	*v.*	(formal) to stop happening or existing; to stop sth. from happening or existing （使）停止，终止，结束
precedence /ˈpresɪdəns/	*n.*	the condition of being more important than sb. else and therefore coming or being dealt with first 优先，优先权
interpersonal /ˌɪntəˈpɜːsənl/	*a.*	connected with relationships between people 人际关系的，人际的
surpass /səˈpɑːs/	*v.*	(formal) to do or be better than sb./sth. 超过，胜过，优于
suppress /səˈpres/	*v.*	to prevent yourself from having or expressing a feeling or an emotion 抑制，控制，忍住
unmet /ˌʌnˈmet/	*a.*	(formal) (of needs, etc.) not satisfied （需要等）未满足的
policy /ˈpɒləsi/	*n.*	a written statement of a contract of insurance 保险单
pharmaceutical /ˌfɑːməˈsuːtɪkl/	*a.*	connected with making and selling drugs and medicines 制药的，配药的，卖药的

English for Marketing

 **Exercises**

Exercise 1. Language: Fill in the blanks with words or expressions from the above article.

1. _____ manufacturers develop and sell medicines that can cure diseases, hence they can satisfy people's safety needs.
2. Insurance _____, especially life insurance ones, which compensate for people's severe loss in financial form, bring strong sense of safety to them.
3. If physiological needs are _____, people will be less likely to pursue needs of higher level.
4. If deficiency needs are not met, consumers will have to _____ his desire of self-actualization activities.
5. She had to learn that her wishes did not take _____ over other people's needs.
6. Since it is a natural need for human beings to socialize, we should learn how to deal with _____ relationships with people around us.
7. Maslow's Hierarchy of Needs is so _____ that many disciplines adopt it as a model to analyze people's needs.
8. Everybody in the marketing department is aware that the department cannot _____ well without sufficient support from other departments within the company.
9. Researchers argue that it is impossible that human beings should satisfy their needs level by level as _____ processes run at the same time in the human brains.
10. The new product under development is anticipated to _____ consumers expectations once it is launched.

Exercise 2. Knowledge: True or false statements. If the following statements are true, write T; if false, write F.

1. The human brain is a complex system and has unparallel processes running at the same time. ( )
2. Physiological needs such as water, food are the physical requirements for human survival. ( )
3. Deficiency needs include needs for esteem, friendship, love, security, and physiological needs. ( )
4. A product that is developed to address a non-existent problem is meaningless. ( )
5. Social needs may overcome the physiological and security needs depending on the strength of the peer pressure. ( )
6. The insurance policy can be used as a way to satisfy a customer's esteem needs. ( )

7. Self-actualization needs can be satisfied by earning as much as possible.　　（　）
8. Being trained for a marathon for the first time is a kind of social needs.　　（　）
9. Finding a shelter to stay is an aspect of physiological needs.　　（　）
10. Joining a golf club is a way to satisfy one's physiological needs.　　（　）

Exercise 3. Language: Translate the following sentences into Chinese.

1. It should be noted that the development of every product or service should be based on real customer needs.

2. Only by carefully observing consumers' basic needs and changing needs can marketers spot any future business opportunities.

3. You are advised to read the fine print of motor insurance policies carefully before signing.

4. Once a person's physiological needs are relatively satisfied, his/her safety needs may take precedence and dominate behaviors.

5. People with low self-esteem often crave for respect from others and more interested in seeking fame or glory.

6. They need to communicate and establish their interpersonal relationships with people around them.

7. In order to help satisfy people need for esteem and respect, many companies develop products of higher quality and of course, higher price.

8. Maslow's Hierarchy of Needs is often portrayed in the shape of a pyramid with the most fundamental needs at the bottom, and the need for self-actualization at the top.

9. It is said that the success of every company is dependent on its ability to create products and services that address unmet customer needs.

   _____

   _____

10. The need for self-actualization refers to what a person's full potential is and the realization of that potential.

    _____

    _____

Oral practice: Discuss the following topic with your partners and report your findings to the class orally.

Can you list some of the products that can meet customers' needs in different categories one by one? For example, products that can satisfy safety needs include: locks, insurance...

Text C: Extensive Reading

Learning Resources

How to Differentiate Between Wants & Needs

By Sean McPheat

Do you know what the difference is between a need and a want?

A lot of people think that they are the same but indeed they are different. When selling it's important that you understand the difference between needs and wants because you need to appeal to both during the sales interaction.

And understanding this element of sales is always one of the most important areas that any Sales Training course will cover.

Let's take a closer look.

What is the difference between needs and wants?

Look at needs as those things that are vital for survival and a want is something that you desire. Wants are almost always linked to an emotion that the want gives you.

You need food to survive right? But why do you have that expensive cut of steak? The answer is that you want it, you'll love the taste, maybe how it looks and if you're on a date then you want to impress your partner. They are all wants.

The need would be to put calories in your body for survival. The want is everything else.

When a want and a need are aligned then you have a lay down sale!

In terms of selling, think of needs as MUST-HAVE-DO-OR-DIE criteria. These MUST be fulfilled. Wants are everything else.

When selling to someone listen very closely to the language that they use because it will reveal all and what is most important to them.

Here's an example:

"The car needs to have 4 doors because of my kids and also Bluetooth because I travel a lot and want to sync my phone with the stereo. It must be economical too because I travel in excess of 20,000 miles per annum to and from work. Bit of poke would be nice and I'd like heated seats and a wireless charger."

Now let's take a look.

The MUST-HAVE-DO-OR-DIE items were:

Four doors;

Bluetooth;

Miles per gallon.

These MUST be fulfilled first before anything else so as a salesperson these would be your go to items to cover off before you look at the others items which were nice to have wants.

They were:

A bit of poke;

Heated seats;

Wireless charger.

So those 3 items could be negotiated but the 3 must-have items would not be. Now if you had a car to sell with all 6 features then it should be one of those lay down sales that I mentioned earlier as long as the price was right.

If you had the 3 must-have items and say 2 of the nice-to-have items then you could have a sale if you included something else.

Uncovering the Customers' Needs and Wants

Imagine that you need a car to get to work each day and to drop the kids off at school. So, you've made the decision to buy a car because you NEED it.

But the brand, the make and the model that you choose will be based on your WANTS. If it was a simple as getting from A to B then everyone would be driving low-cost cars that did the job.

But purchasing decisions are not made like that!

That's a really good example of grasping the difference between customer needs and wants and is one that I recommend that you take into your selling interactions.

Normally the decision is made to buy in order to fulfil a need. Your job as a salesperson is to cater for their wants and this is where the majority of your focus should be.

That doesn't mean ramming benefits and features down the customer's throat. Customers hate to be sold to but they love to buy. Give the customer a good listening to.

So how can you elicit the customer needs and wants? Well, it all comes down to the quality of your questioning and listening skills.

Consultative selling skills are a must when it comes down to understanding needs and wants. It's not a one-way sales-pitch here. Instead you should be asking lots of questions around why they want something, how they want it, the impact it will have on them and what's important when they make decisions like this.

And what they don't want is as important as understanding what they do want. Your customer may have made purchasing decisions in the past and have got their fingers burned.

"And I don't want the payment protection cover because I've never made a claim in over 20 years so I've been wasting my money."

Now imagine a sales person trying to convince this customer that they do need it? It will probably come over as pushy and that it is in the self-interest of the salesperson's commission rather than what the customer wants.

Some people have fears about what will happen in their business if they don't achieve their goals. By helping them move away from those situations, you lessen the fears and help them build confidence.

Others have opportunities to achieve goals and they need help to move towards them. This is a chance for you to discuss the gains they would get from your products and services.

Never Sell Anything Unless you Understand Their Needs and Wants

"Prescription before diagnosis is malpractice." It's an old but good cliché. Your doctor wouldn't prescribe medicine or drugs without first asking you lots of questions around your symptoms and situation. The same can be applicable to selling. Never sell anything without first understanding the customers' needs and wants.

You can then tailor your interaction with them on the areas that are most important to them. Not the areas that are most important to you.　(945 words)

Writing: Read the article carefully and write a brief summary of it. Your summary should include the following information: the definition of needs and wants, the differences between them, and how to promote sales of your products by taking advantage of this knowledge.

Word limit: 300 words.

Unit 13

Customer Loyalty

Quote of the Unit:

"If people believe they share values with a company, they will stay loyal to the brand."

—Howard Schultz, CEO of Starbucks

Learning Objectives:

1. Understand the basic concept of customer loyalty.
2. Understand the benefits of winning customer loyalty.
3. Understand different types of customer loyalty and how to build them.
4. Master the language used in discussing customer loyalty issues.

Pre-class Questions:

1. According to your understanding, what is customer loyalty?
2. Do you know the possible benefits of having loyal customers?
3. Do you know any loyalty schemes incorporated by some brands that you know? How effective these loyalty schemes are?

Text A: Lead-in

Learning Resources

How to Build Customer Loyalty?

Customer loyalty is the **measurement** of a customer's willingness to stay with one brand.

Building customer loyalty is particularly important for improving the lifetime value of current customers, which can make up most of the company's revenue.

There are two major types of customer loyalty. The first is **transactional** loyalty, and the second is **emotional** loyalty.

How to Build Transactional Customer Loyalty

This type of loyalty is **rational** in nature. There is no emotional connection in transactional loyalty and it is based on factors such as convenience, low prices, gifts, availability of products, etc. If any of those conditions change, customers will look for other brands as a **replacement**. Certain industries, including **pharmacies**, gas stations, and grocery stores put great emphasis on creating transactional loyalty to grow business.

There are many ways to generate transactional loyalty. Below are some of the principles of designing transactional loyalty schemes.

Loss aversion: An interesting fact: customers care more about potential loss than gain. By incorporating loyalty schemes that provide rewards, points, and bonuses you can encourage customers to maintain business relationship with you, since otherwise they'll lose the points they have earned from you.

Recency bias: Customers may see 100+ ads a day but barely remember any, but only some impactful and mostly the recent ones stay on top of mind. Brands can take advantage of this effect by by ensuring the beginnings and ends of ads are positive and appealing.

Reciprocity: Reciprocity is a well-documented social norm where people respond to a positive action with another positive one. Brands can create transactional loyalty by leading with value, such as a gift or credit, which can spur customers to respond.

How to Build Emotional Customer Loyalty

The second type is emotional loyalty, or loyalty based on customers' positive emotions associated with the brand. This kind of loyalty is not built on incentives such as offers and other rewards, but rather on trust, storytelling, customer service, and philanthropy. Emotional loyalty is what makes customers choose your brand above others regardless of price, convenience, or any other factors.

In this case, the brand has either become part of the customer's identity, or a way to express his/her identity. Because of this, they are much less likely to be influenced by competing offers and brands may be less subject to price elasticity of demand.

Emotional loyalty makes customers feel like they are a part of the brand and they become ambassadors because they want others to feel the same.

There are many famous examples of brands that have created emotional loyalty with customers. Here are some of them.

TOMS Shoes

Since its inception, TOMS built a brand and business model on the foundation of giving: for every pair of shoes purchased from TOMS, a pair is donated to a child in need. Though they may not be the cheapest pair of shoes, consumers are more willing to spend the additional money on TOMS because of what it gives away.

According to research, when customers build emotional connections with such brands, they are more likely to visit their stores and spend more money for their products or services.

Dove's Self Esteem Project

Dove is one of the most recognizable beauty brands in the world. Instead of saying which Dove product will make women beautiful, they set their marketing campaign around the idea that women should recognize that they are already beautiful. Dove wanted to rid women of the anxiety and insecurities they face every day, so their campaign aimed at how beautiful women can be regardless of their size, color, or shape.

This campaign has definitely established and increased trust between Dove and women. The brand makes women feel good about themselves, which in turn, makes them feel good about the brand. Hence, female customers are emotionally connected with the brand.

Coca-Cola

Over the last century, Coca-Cola has done a great job of consistently fostering positive emotions through its advertising campaigns: whether it's Santa Claus, a polar bear, or an individual person, they're always drinking a Coke and show the world their happiness as they smile, beam and laugh.

In contrast, its major rival's messaging is always telling us about how much better it is when comparing with Coke. Coke, on the other hand, rarely mentions its competition. Its major rival is trying to convey its messages to the rational/behavioral customer, while Coca-Cola's advertising campaigns evoke **positivity** with "Taste the Feeling" or "Open Happiness". This can connect the brand with customers who align themselves with its values emotionally. (756 words)

Vocabulary and Useful Expressions

measurement	/ˈmeʒəmənt/	n.	The measurement of the quality, value, or effect of something is the activity of deciding how great it is. （质量、价值或影响的）衡量，评估，估量
transactional	/trænˈzækʃənəl/	a.	relating to the conducting of business, especially buying or selling 交易的
emotional	/ɪˈməʊʃənl/	a.	connected with people's feelings (= with the emotions) 感情的，情感的，情绪的
rational	/ˈræʃnəl/	a.	(of behaviour, ideas, etc.) based on reason rather than emotions （行为、思想等）合理的，理性的，明智的
replacement	/rɪˈpleɪsmənt/	n.	a thing that replaces sth., especially because the first thing is old, broken, etc. 替代品，替换物
pharmacy	/ˈfɑːməsɪ/	n.	a shop/store, or part of one, that sells medicines and drugs 药房，药店，医药柜台
aversion	/əˈvɜːʃn/	n.	a strong feeling of not liking sb./sth. (~ to sb./sth.) 厌恶，憎恶
recency	/ˈriːsnsɪ/	n.	the property of having happened or appeared not long ago（as in primacy-recency effect，首因－近因效应）近因
reciprocity	/ˌresɪˈprɒsətɪ/	n.	(formal) a situation in which two people, countries, etc. provide the same help or advantages to each other 互惠，互助，互换
positivity	/ˌpɒzɪˈtɪvɪtɪ/	n.	the practice of being or tendency to be positive or optimistic in attitude 积极性

1. *Price Elasticity of Demand*: a measurement of the change in the consumption of a product in relation to a change in its price.

Expressed mathematically, it is: Price Elasticity of Demand = Percentage of Change in Quantity Demanded/Percentage of Change in Price

Economists use price elasticity to understand how supply and demand for a product change when its price changes. A good is elastic if a price change causes a substantial change in demand or supply. A good is inelastic if a price change does not cause demand or supply to change very much. The availability of a substitute for a product affects its elasticity. If there are no good substitutes and the product is necessary, demand won't change when the price goes up, making it inelastic.

2. *Primacy and Recency Effect*: It (also known as the serial-position effect) is the tendency to recall the first and the last items in a series well, and the middle ones poorly. There's no consensus as to why this phenomenon occurs but it does exist.

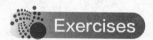

Exercise 1. Language: Fill in the blanks with words or expressions from the above article.

1. Don't promote negativity online and expect people to treat you with _____ in person.
2. The Consumer Protection Act stipulates that customers must be made aware of the _____ charges associated with their purchases.
3. A point-based reward system leads to transactions but doesn't necessarily strengthen emotional _____.
4. Consumers typically have an _____ to potential loss.
5. We offer to all our trading partners a commitment to _____ and fairness.
6. If the product doesn't work, you are given the choice of a refund or a new product for _____.
7. A typical independent _____ that mainly sells medicine gets 90% of its income from prescriptions.
8. Though many buying decisions are on _____ basis, it is not rare that consumers make emotional buying decisions in a hasty manner.
9. Customer loyalty is the _____ of customer's intention to stay with a brand/company.

10. _____ effect is a psychological phenomenon and cognitive bias that is often used in sales and marketing to influence the customer decision making process.

Exercise 2. Knowledge: Discuss with your partners and answer the following questions.

1. How many types of customer loyalty are there according to the article?

2. According to your understanding, what measures can a company take to boost transactional loyalty among its customer base?

3. According to your understanding, what measures can a company take to boost emotional loyalty among its customer base?

Exercise 3. Knowledge: True or false statements. If the following statements are ture, write T; if false, write F.

1. Recency bias refers to the fact that consumers tend to pay more attention to the beginning of an ad and are influenced by the first impression. ( )
2. Loss aversion refers to the fact that consumers hate to suffer from a potential loss. ( )
3. Coca-Cola succeeded in winning emotional loyalty partly because it insists on creating positive images in its advertising campaigns. ( )
4. In Dove's Self Esteem Project, it encourages women to face themselves positively and accept who they are. ( )
5. TOMS tries to connect the brand with its customers emotionally by committing itself to philanthropy. ( )
6. By resorting to reciprocity to create transactional loyalty, a brand may often send gifts or credits to customers to evoke response. ( )
7. The creation of transactional loyalty normally relies on factors such as convenience, gifts, low prices, availability of products, etc. ( )
8. Emotional loyalty is often created on the basis of incentives such as offers and other rewards. ( )
9. It is necessary to build trust between customers and a brand so that customers may feel connected by the brand emotionally.
10. Storytelling is also one important factor in creating emotional loyalty: good story that carries positive values will appeal to customers. ( )

Text B: Intensive Reading

Customer Loyalty

Learning Resources

It is commonly believed that customer loyalty plays a significant role in the development of one business.

Being loyal means being firm and not changing in your support for a person, a product, a company, an organization or a brand.

Customer loyalty refers to the tendency to repurchase a particular product, service or brand or revisit a particular company shop or website many times. Those who keep buying the same product or products from the same brand must be loyal customers.

Those who keep visiting the same website or shop, for example, a particular shop on Taobao, can also be regarded as loyal customers. Customer loyalty is very critical to business success and profitability.

In other words, loyal customers play a very important role in the development of one business. It is estimated that 20% of the customers, who tend to be loyal, tend to contribute to 80% of the total profits of one business.

Loyal customers tend to buy more and buy more expensive products. They tend to repeat purchase with the same brand many times. They are also willing to introduce their favorite brands to friends, colleagues and relatives, causing the so-called **de facto** viral marketing.

But nowadays, loyalty is very precious, since customers are becoming more and more **fickle**.

In this context, being fickle means being not firm in one's support for a brand or a company.

Why are people more and more fickle? Why do they not hesitate to switch brands frequently? One critical reason is that consumers have increasingly more and more options to choose from. The market is now **saturated** with many homogeneous products. They may have similar appearance, similar design, similar functions and similar **configuration**. Maybe the only difference between them is the price. Hence, people tend to have difficulty in making a decision.

And since technological innovation is particularly fast, new products from new companies appear very quickly and frequently. Therefore, the market witnesses a generation of fickle customers.

Under such circumstances, companies have to face double problems: profit margin is **shrinking**; customer loyalty is decreasing. Hence, customer loyalty becomes particularly precious, and how to win back customer loyalty becomes an urgent and realistic issue for companies. Marketers should try to figure out ways to encourage customer loyalty to boost sales and increase profitability. Great attention is given to marketing and customer service to retain current customers by increasing their customer loyalty.

They also resort to the development and implementation of loyalty programs which reward customers for repeat business. Loyalty programs are structured marketing strategies designed by merchants to encourage customers to continue to shop at or use the services of businesses associated with each program.

These programs exist covering most types of business each one having varying features and reward schemes. In marketing generally and in retailing more specifically, a loyalty card, rewards card, points card, advantage card, or club card is a plastic or paper card, visually similar to a credit card, debit card, or digital card that identifies the card holder as a member in a loyalty program. Loyalty cards (both physical and digital) relate to the loyalty business model.

By presenting such a card purchasers typically earn the right either to a discount on the current purchase or to an allotment of points that they can use for future purchases.

Hence the card is the visible means of implementing a type of what economists call a two-part tariff where a customer has provided sufficient identifying information.

The loyalty card may also be used to access information to **expedite verification** during receipt of cheques or **dispensing** medical **prescription** preparations or for other membership **privileges**, such as gaining access to a club **lounge** in airports by using a frequent-flyer card. B2B (business-to-business) loyalty programs reward businesses for their purchase of goods and services from suppliers.

Loyalty cards are becoming mobile. There has been a move away from traditional magnetic card, stamp or punchcard based on schemes to online and mobile on-line loyalty programs. While these schemes vary, the common element is a push toward elimination of a traditional card in favour of an electronic **equivalent**.

The choice of medium is often a QR code. The most **prominent** examples: WeChat and Alipay mobile Apps in China and the world across.

These two Apps allow business to associate the loyalty programs with them and by simply scanning the QR code or just one purchase experience at the store the users can obtain the virtual membership card of that brand or store, allowing them to enter the loyalty programs.

In these cases sometimes the users need to input more personal information and sometimes do not need to do so, because these Apps may allow the loyalty programs to access to the prestored personal information.

And every time the user purchases, he can show the mobile loyalty card to the shop assistant to enjoy a discount or get loyalty points. Sometimes the Apps can automatically make reduction of the original pricing by activating the membership.

At the same time, the Apps can automatically push some discount information to users luring them to become more loyal to the brand. At the end of a certain period, say, one fiscal year, the customer can redeem the points in the loyalty card for some coupons, vouchers and even gifts directly. Though loyalty programs are widely adopted, in order to boost customer loyalty and increase sales there are companies complaining that these loyalty programs discount goods to people that are buying their goods anyway, and that the expense of doing these programs rarely show a good return on the investment.

Other critics see the lower prices and rewards as **bribes** to manipulate customer loyalty and purchasing decisions, or in the case of infrequent spenders, a means of **subsidizing** them.

And some consumer privacy watchers warn that commercial use of the personal data collected as part of the schemes has the potential for **abuse**.

It is highly likely that consumer purchases are tracked and used for marketing research to increase the efficiency of marketing and advertising; in fact, this can be one of the purposes of the loyalty card. Nevertheless, facing weakening customer loyalty and shrinking profit margin, loyalty program is still regarded as one efficient solution.   (1040 words)

Vocabulary and Useful Expressions

de facto /ˌdeɪ ˈfæktəʊ/	a.	(from Latin, formal) existing as a fact although it may not be legally accepted as existing （常用于名词前）实际上存在的（不一定合法）
fickle /ˈfɪkl/	a.	(of a person) often changing their mind in an unreasonable way so that you cannot rely on them （人）反复无常的

saturated	/ˈsætʃəreɪtɪd/	a.	if the market for a product is saturated, there is more of the product available than there are people who want to buy it （市场）饱和的
configuration	/kənˌfɪɡəˈreɪʃn/	n.	the way in which something, such as a computer system or software, is organized to operate 配置
shrink	/ʃrɪŋk/	v.	to become or to make sth. smaller in size or amount （使）缩小，收缩，减少
expedite	/ˈekspədaɪt/	v.	(formal) to make a process happen more quickly 加快，加速
verification	/ˌverɪfɪˈkeɪʃn/	n.	the process of establishing the truth, accuracy, or validity of something 验证
dispense	/dɪˈspens/	v.	When a chemist dispenses medicine, he or she prepares it, and gives or sells it to the patient or customer. 配（药），配（方），发（药）
prescription	/prɪˈskrɪpʃn/	n.	medicine that your doctor has ordered for you 医生开的药
privilege	/ˈprɪvəlɪdʒ/	n.	a special right or advantage that a particular person or group of people has 特殊利益，优惠待遇
lounge	/laʊndʒ/	n.	a room for waiting in at an airport, etc. （机场等的）等候室
equivalent	/ɪˈkwɪvələnt/	n.	a thing, amount, word, etc. that is equivalent to sth. else (~ of/to sth.) 相等的东西，等量，对应词
prominent	/ˈprɒmɪnənt/	a.	something that is prominent is very noticeable or is an important part of something else 显著的，突出的，引人注目的
bribe	/braɪb/	n.	a sum of money or sth. valuable that you give or offer to sb. to persuade them to help you, especially by doing sth. dishonest 贿赂
subsidize	/ˈsʌbsɪdaɪz/	v.	to give money to sb. or an organization to help pay for sth.; to give a subsidy 资助，补助，给……发津贴
abuse	/əˈbjuːs; əˈbjuːz/	n.	the use of sth. in a way that is wrong or harmful (~ of sth.) 滥用，妄用

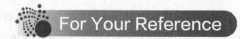
For Your Reference

Viral marketing or viral advertising is a business strategy that uses existing social networks to promote a product mainly on various social media platforms. Its name refers to how consumers spread information about a product with other people, much in the same way that a virus spreads from one person to another. It can be delivered by word of mouth, or enhanced by the network effects of the Internet and mobile networks.

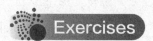
Exercises

Exercise 1. Language: Fill in the blanks with words or expressions from the above article.

1. China highly values ecological and environmental protection. Guided by the conviction that lucid waters and lush mountains are invaluable assets, the country advocates harmonious coexistence between humans and nature, and thus governments of different levels encourage and _____ environment-friendly projects.
2. If the customer feels really bad about one brand, he/she may not hesitate to _____ to another good brand.
3. According to the agreement, a registered member can enjoy all the benefits and _____ of club membership.
4. Service stations use petrol as a bait to _____ motorists into the restaurants and other facilities.
5. The company has recently launched a loyalty App, which can be regarded as an electronic _____ of its loyalty cared.
6. The company denied the accusation that it had been involved in any attempt to _____ the market.
7. Some critics hold that low prices and rewards are just _____ offered to court customers.
8. The consumer electronics market is highly _____, which means the market is highly competitive, and thus forces companies to invest more into R&D to develop products with innovative functions and higher quality to compete in the market.
9. If you carefully examine the market, you'll find out that the market is currently full of _____ products that are very similar to each other.
10. If the customers are _____, they may not stay with a brand for very long and are always ready to _____ from one brand to another.
11. The size of the PC market is expected to _____ in next quarter, considering the fact that more and more people opt for laptop computers which are more convenient

to carry around.
12. The company has developed rapid order processing system to _____ deliveries to customers to improve customer satisfaction in terms of timely delivery.
13. The company, occupying two thirds of the PC market in this country, enjoys _____ leadership though it is not officially announced and recognized.
14. The new housing developments are _____ landmarks in this remote area.
15. The prices of PC in this store range from RMB 2,000 yuan to 10,000 yuan, depending on the particular _____.

Exercise 2. Knowledge: Discuss with your partners and answer the following questions.

1. According to your observation, why are consumers in the new millennium less likely to become loyal to certain brands?

   _____
   _____

2. According to your understanding, which type of business enjoys a relatively higher customer loyalty? What drives customer loyalty in this case?

   _____
   _____

3. According to your understanding, which type of business suffers from very weak customer loyalty? What may be the factors that lead to this weak loyalty?

   _____
   _____

4. Many companies develop loyalty programs or schemes to offer rewards or points to attract consumers to adhere to their business. Under such circumstances, what type of customer loyalty do these companies attempt to create? Emotional loyalty or transactional loyalty?

   _____
   _____

5. As mentioned in the article, it is a trend that more and more companies try to integrate their loyalty programs with popular mobile Apps such as WeChat and Alipay in different ways. What do you think may be the benefits of doing so? What may be the potential disadvantages or threats? List both of them.

   _____
   _____

Exercise 3. Language: Match the words from Column A with those from Column B.

Column A	Column B
1. homogeneous	A. purchase
2. saturated	B. information
3. dispense	C. products
4. membership	D. privileges
5. prestored	E. prescriptions
6. fickle	F. market
7. prominent	G. market position
8. de facto	H. customers
9. manipulate	I. leadership
10. repeat	J. loyalty

Oral practice: Discuss with your partners. Think about the reasons why a consumer may become loyal to a brand, or why a consumer may defect from a brand that he used to be loyal to. You may list the reasons and classify them into different categories. You are expected to use both the language and knowledge learned in this unit. Your product of this discussion should be a written list of the reasons.

Text C: Extensive Reading

Learning Resources

Two Cases of Customer Loyalty Creation

How Costco Creates Customer Loyalty

Costco Wholesale Corporation is the largest American membership-only warehouse club. It has been aggressively infiltrating global markets with retail innovation practices that have created a cult-like consumer following characterized as "The Costco Craze". In 2021, the company has achieved a sales volume of up to 192 billion dollars making it a fantastic case for study on customer loyalty.

As their management states in their latest 10-Q[1] filing, 2021:

"We believe the most important driver of our profitability is sales growth, particularly comparable warehouse sales growth... Comparable sales growth is achieved through increasing shopping frequency from new and existing members and the amount they spend on each visit (average ticket)."

1. Cross Subsidizing with a Membership Model

Costco's loyalty program begins with their membership business model.

Members pay an upfront cost to be able to enter the store and purchase goods. In return, Costco provides low, competitive prices, private label items, and other exclusive perks.

"Our membership format is an integral part of our business model and has a significant effect on our profitability. This format is designed to reinforce member loyalty and provide continuing fee revenue." — Costco 10-Q, 2021

2. Using Loss Leaders to Promote Transactional Loyalty

Part of Costco's loyalty strategy is to "provide members with quality goods and services at the most competitive prices". Instead of maximizing profits per transaction, they focus on maximizing each customer's lifetime value to the company.

This is exemplified most clearly in their gasoline service. Though the gasoline business has a significantly lower gross margin percentage relative to their non-gasoline business, it draws members, and hence gives rise to its customer base.

Costco takes measures to ensure members will always save on their gas bill. They are able to do this because of their membership business model, which doesn't rely on profits in gasoline to fuel the business.

3. Using Unique, Private Label Products to Increase Loyalty

Private label products increase customer loyalty in a number of ways.

First, it distinguishes Costco from other competitors. Instead of competing in products, Costco

---

[1] SEC Form 10-Q is a comprehensive report of financial performance that must be submitted quarterly by all public companies to the Securities and Exchange Commission (SEC). In the 10-Q, firms are required to disclose relevant information regarding their finances as a result of their business operations. The 10-Q is generally an unaudited report.

can offer exclusive options for their members.

Further, as customers become "addicted" to these products, it improves their membership retention rate. If customers want to enjoy these products, they must continue shopping at Costco.

Because of the exclusivity, these products are often more profitable on a unit basis as well.

4. Maximize Loss Leaders with Creative Financing Options

Finally, Costco complements their product offering with a branded credit card. They have tailored the rewards card to maximize customer loyalty, highlighting some of the biggest reasons to be a member such as:
- 4% cash back on Costco gas;
- 2% cash back on Costco purchases.

How Starbucks Improves Customer Loyalty

Starbucks is another premier case for study on how to improve customer loyalty.

1. Cross Channel Marketing

Starbucks does an incredible job driving customers into their loyalty program.

Starbucks adopted an omni-channel strategy that takes advantage of multiple channels, all leading to subscriptions to its renowned loyalty program.

Once subscribed to its e-mail list, customers will receive member exclusive offers. If they would like to partake, they must enroll in the loyalty program.

Starbucks extends their rewards program to lower margin grocery items as well. The rewards themselves help drive traffic to their in-store locations, increasing frequency, lifetime value, and accessing a whole new group of customers.

2. New Product Development

Starbucks also drives repeat purchases through new product development.

With a steady stream of new options, customers are nudged to come back and try their latest creations. These new products often embody other aspects of the business, in this case Starbucks' relationship with Oatly.

"We recognize that we are a beverage-forward concept. Beverage is our key point of differentiation." — Pat Grismer

3. Create Urgency with Limited-time Offers

Additionally, seasonal holiday beverages create excitement in their customer base and provides a sense of urgency to come into the store.

In fact, there are now many seasonal beverages that customers pine for, including Pumpkin Spice Latte, Peppermint Mocha, and Irish Cream Cold Brews.

Further, Starbucks constantly rotates in limited run premium products.

Combined, holiday and limited time products give a reason to return.

4. Unique Experiences for Rewards Members

Finally, Starbucks routinely creates rewards member engagement campaigns. These often take the form of exclusive games and rewards Starbucks rewards members can participate in.

Here is just one example. In Starbucks for life, rewards members collect game pieces that can earn them rewards ranging from a $500 gift card, Bose Earbuds, and of course, the namesake grand price, free Starbucks for life.

In both cases, at its core, customer loyalty is about providing a better experience. While there are many ways to improve customer's experience in an e-commerce context, the primary ways revolve around creating personalized, relevant experiences and offers across all channels as illustrated by the above cases.   (868 words)

(**Source:** https://www.barilliance.com/customer-loyalty-programs/#t-1615482611722.)

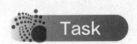

Writing: Try to search for successful examples of companies creating and improving customer loyalty. Select one of them and write a short report on how the company succeeded in improving customer loyalty—be it transactional loyalty or emotional loyalty. You are encouraged to write down some of the measures taken methodically, by using both the language and knowledge learned in this unit. As for format, you can refer to the above article.

Word limit: 500 words.

Unit 14

Customer Relationship Management

Quote of the Unit:

"Strong customer relationships drive sales, sustainability, and growth."

—Tom Cates, chairman and founder of the Brookeside Group

Learning Objectives:

1. Understand the most important functionalities of CRM systems.
2. Understand the most important benefits of implementing CRM systems.
3. Understand the most frequently used terms and concepts in discussing CRM.
4. Use both the knowledge and language learned to discuss issues related to CRM.

Pre-class Questions:

1. What problems can cause marketers to lose customers?
2. How can marketers and sales force identify high-value customers?
3. How can customer service representatives better serve customer?

Text A: Lead-in

Why You Need a CRM Tool

Learning Resources

By intelligently storing and managing your customers' information, a CRM system increases the number of leads coming in, helping your marketing team find new customers faster. It supports your sales teams in closing more deals faster. It also enhances customer service. For example, by adding customer data to your customer service software, contact center agents are better able to meet the customers' needs in a more **engaging**, productive, and efficient manner.

Here are eight signs indicating the need to think about implementing a CRM system.

1. Sales is a struggle.

At some point, all companies need to enter new markets or introduce new products. But if you are struggling to keep up with the business you are generating now, you might need to invest in an integrated CRM solution. A CRM can sort, analyze, and **prioritize** your sales leads so that your sales team can focus on the opportunities that are likely to close and provide accurate answers to customers — quickly and efficiently — and your customer service team has the information they need for upselling and cross-selling.

2. Customer profiles are difficult to build.

If you cannot locate all your customer data points, all you can do is guess when it comes time to build your ideal customer profile. Not only that, you will have no visibility into your sales team's activities. To find out this information, you will have to hold more status meetings, taking your salespeople away from customers and **exacerbating** the issue.

3. Customer service is not good.

Is your customer retention rate slipping?

Do you have an **abysmal** net promoter score (NPS)?

Are contact center handle times in the **stratosphere**?

What is your average first response time?

If your customer service reps are reacting to customer issues and not **proactively** working with customers, it is time to invest in a CRM tool for your service team, one that can give you a unified view of your customer so that reps can offer spectacular service.

4. Marketing and sales departments aren't collaborating.

Since a good CRM can hold all types of information, it can be the rallying point for different teams. A lack of cooperation between departments is the source of many customer pain points. They're forced to repeat themselves. Promises made to them slip through the cracks. No one seems to know their history. Without smooth cooperation between all teams, customers will leave.

Aligning business processes between sales, customer service, marketing, and even some back-office roles (such as billing, inventory, or logistics) is a tricky affair. But if all the components of a CRM share a common data model, all employees can access, use, and add data. They can work collaboratively and share insights, leads, issues, and purchase history. When information is shared across teams, productivity and efficiency skyrocket, data **silos** disappear, and your entire company appears as one **cohesive** unit to the customer.

5. High-value accounts are unknown.

You don't want your best customers to feel unappreciated, but that is hard if you don't know who those customers are. The right CRM tool can identify them so that any customer-facing employee can acknowledge them, provide the right incentives, and nurture them to increase customer loyalty.

6. Contacts within an account cannot be identified.

CRM solutions can help keep track of contacts within a business, to allow both sales and marketing teams to personalize communication. Good CRM solutions can supplement their account and contact data through third-party data sources so that all information is complete and up to date. So, if a contact has moved to a new job, your sales, service, and marketing teams know about it, allowing them to maintain and rebuild these important relationships.

7. Customer data is incomplete or inaccurate.

Incomplete and dirty data is a big issue for brands worldwide. Good CRM solutions automatically flow second- and third-party account and contact information into your CRM system, filling in missing information that salespeople left out and intelligently removing **duplicates**.

8. Forecasting and reporting is difficult.

If reports are still produced by downloading data into spreadsheets, they are taking way too much time to create and are probably inaccurate. Inaccurate reports lead to faulty planning and forecasting. While time-consuming administrative tasks keep your sales team from doing what they should be doing — selling. A good CRM system keeps data in one centrally located, easily accessible place, making accurate, real-time reporting and forecasting easy.　　(737 words)

(**Source:** https://www.oracle.com/cx/what-is-crm/why-crm-is-important/.)

Vocabulary and Useful Expressions

engaging /ɪnˈɡeɪdʒɪŋ/	*a.*	interesting or pleasant in a way that attracts your attention　有趣的，令人愉快的，迷人的
prioritize /praɪˈɒrətaɪz/	*v.*	to put tasks, problems, etc. in order of importance, so that you can deal with the most important first　按重要性排列，划分优先顺序
exacerbate /ɪɡˈzæsəbeɪt/	*v.*	(formal) to make sth. worse, especially a disease or problem　使恶化，使加剧，使加重
abysmal /əˈbɪzməl/	*a.*	extremely bad or of a very low standard　极坏的，糟透的
stratosphere /ˈstrætəsfɪə(r)/	*n.*	If you say that someone or something climbs or is sent into the stratosphere, you mean that they reach a very high level.　最高层，最高水平，顶峰（原意：平流层）
proactively /ˌprəʊˈæktɪvlɪ/	*ad.*	controlling a situation in a way that makes things happen rather than waiting for things to happen and then reacting to them　积极主动地，主动出击地，先发制人地
silo /ˈsaɪləʊ/	*n.*	a tall tower on a farm used for storing grain, etc.　筒仓
cohesive /kəʊˈhiːsɪv/	*a.*	forming a united whole　结成一个整体的
duplicate /ˈdjuːplɪkeɪt/	*n.*	one of two or more things that are the same in every detail　完全一样的东西，复制品，副本

1. *Upselling* is when a salesperson offers an upgrade or premium version of the product they are selling. Upselling can also include offering add-ons to increase the functionality of the product. The goal of upselling is to increase the total sale and to introduce customers to options that might better suit their needs.
2. *Cross-selling* is suggesting the customer buy a related product or service. For example, a housekeeping service agent might cross-sell by also offering a carpet deep cleaning service.
3. A *data silo* is a repository of data that's controlled by one department or business unit and isolated from the rest of an organization, much like grass and grain in a farm silo are closed off from outside elements. Siloed data typically is stored in a standalone system and often is incompatible with other data sets.

Exercise 1. Language: Fill in the blanks with words or expressions from the above article.

1. What can a CRM do for the sales team: a CRM can _____, _____ and _____ your sales leads so that your sales team can focus on the opportunities.
2. When it comes to building ideal customer profile: a CRM can help _____ all your customer data points.
3. When it comes to customer service: a CRM can provide a _____ view of your customer so that customer service reps can offer spectacular service.
4. When it comes to personalized communication: CRM solutions can help _____ of contacts within a business.
5. When it comes to interdepartmental collaboration: CRM can help _____ business processes between sales, customer service, marketing, and even some back-office roles.
6. When it comes to high-value accounts: a right CRM tool can _____ them so that any customer-facing employee can acknowledge them quickly.
7. When it comes to accurate customer data: CRM solutions can automatically _____ second- and third-party account and contact information into your CRM system, filling in missing information and deleting _____.
8. When it comes to reporting and forecasting: a good CRM system keeps data in one centrally located, easily _____ place, making accurate, real-time reporting and forecasting easy.

Unit 14 Customer Relationship Management

Exercise 2. Knowledge: Answer the following questions briefly according to the above article.

1. *Since a good CRM can hold all types of information, it can be the rallying point for different teams.* In this sentence, what does the term "rallying point" refer to?

   _____
   _____

2. *Incomplete and dirty data is a big issue for brands worldwide.* In this sentence, what does the term "dirty data" refer to?

   _____
   _____

3. *When information is shared across teams, productivity and efficiency skyrocket, data silos disappear, and your entire company appears as one cohesive unit to the customer.* In this sentence, what does the phrase "data silos disappear" refer to?

   _____
   _____

4. *If your customer service reps are reacting to customer issues and not proactively working with customers.* In this sentence, what is the difference between reacting to customers' issues and proactively working with customers? What would be the different results?

   _____
   _____

5. Are contact center handle times in the stratosphere? What does this sentence refer to?

   _____
   _____

6. *Not only that, you will have no visibility into your sales team's activities.* In this sentence, what does the phrase "no visibility into your sales team's activities" refer to?

   _____
   _____

7. *Promises made to them slip through the cracks.* In this sentence, what does the phrase "slip through the cracks" refer to?

   _____
   _____

Text B: Intensive Reading

How to Improve Customer Retention by Using CRM

Learning Resources

As business competition is increasingly fiercer, companies are trying to keep customers engaged with their product more than ever. Many retention strategies have been implemented over time, from VIP memberships and personalizing the customer experience to **re-engaging** customers who are in **hibernation** and upgrading customer service.

A well-implemented CRM system is located at the center of any good retention strategy. The data it collects and the way it integrates with other marketing, sales, and customer service software are crucial to providing your customers with a more personalized experience. Here are a few ways CRM can help retain your customers.

Personalized Experience with CRM Data

The foundation of any relationship is listening and answering with constructive ideas and human compassion. To form a healthy relationship with your customers, you need to be able to regard them as something more than just a source of profit. They are not just letters and numbers with checkmarks on your screen–they are people, and today, people demand **exquisite** service.

CRM data allows you to provide them with that exquisite service by personalizing each campaign, e-mail and contact. Naturally, people will be more interested and engaged if you refer to them by their name and suggest products they really need, as opposed to just **shoving** random ads down their inbox.

Moreover, customers that are engaged will buy up to 90% more often and spend up to 60% more per transaction①. By forming this emotional connection with your brand, they are also five times more likely to shop only with you.

The gathered data will also show who your most valuable customers are. To make them feel special, create loyalty programs that offer **perks** and incentives that will **solidify** your relationship. What's more, **vigilantly** tracking data will help avoid **churn** and thus improve retention.

---

① https://www.alida.com/the-alida-journal/customer-loyalty-stats.

Fully Visible Customer Journey

An in-depth understanding of your customers' needs and wishes is the crucial element for a healthy relationship. The data gathered by CRM software can show you how influential your marketing campaigns are and how your customers are responding to them.

A mapped-out customer journey (as shown in Figure 14.1) shows when and how your customers first interacted with your business, how their engagement phase went, and their post-purchase involvement.

With this data, you can fine-tune your marketing efforts, adjust your sales process up to the point where you lost your customer, or re-engage with a promising client that maybe forgot to renew his membership. Also, cross-selling and upselling is much easier when you have the information on your buyers' interests, frequency of their purchases, and the overall prediction of how much they are ready to spend.

Figure 14.1   A mapped-out customer journey

Source: commons.wikimedia.org.

Transparency Is a Must

One of the best features of CRM software is the ability to set service level agreements, or SLAs for short. With these agreements, you and your customer will always be on the same page. The contents of SLAs are the basic governing principles of a provider-customer relationship. Your customers will feel much safer with this, as they will have a written agreement which exactly states what services you will provide, and how future situations will be handled. As every customer has his own SLA, you can follow the complaints and reply accordingly through CRM.

With a well-defined SLA in place, your customer churn will greatly decrease, since there is almost no chance for missed tickets and late responses.

Case Management

As issues arise, you'll need to be able to handle all the tasks involved in their resolution. Case management helps enable you to:

- store all interactions;
- gather requests;
- track and assign issues;
- monitor the outcomes.

Because the entire system is automated, your team won't have to deal with **mundane** manual tasks, and they can use their time to solve problems and interact with customers.

Case management also helps you manage the previously mentioned SLAs and provides insight into their KPIs.

Integrations

One of the main problems of actual use of a CRM software can be its lack of integration with other tools.

If your team is reluctant to use it, your overall customer experience will suffer, and you will lose customers. There's a whole **palette** of integrations but here we will mention the ones that influence customer experience and retention the most.

E-mail Marketing Integration

An e-mail marketing campaign powered by CRM data is a force to **be reckoned with**. Your campaigns will become highly targeted, as well as automatically analyzed, helping you further **fine-tune** your strategy. This, in turn, will improve your revenue and blacklist tactics that might not be beneficial to your brand.

Marketing integration provides your team with complete communication transparency and a summary grid.

Marketing Automation/Integration

Connecting your marketing and sales teams is the key to creating a **seamless** customer experience. Integrating the two will allow both teams to have access to the same information, saving precious time on lead generation, customer service, and many other processes.

With marketing automation, your CRM data will be instantly updated, or if it's a new prospect, a new account will be created.

Unit 14 Customer Relationship Management

Social Media Integration

Tapping into social media to better your customer service is something you should seriously consider. With Facebook having 1.62 billion daily users, there's a huge chance your customer is one of them. Any social media platform is a valuable medium between the customer and businesses, so not integrating might damage your customer support efficiency.

Concluding Customer Retention

If you want your company to prosper, keeping your existing customers should be one of your primary goals. Retaining customers is much cheaper and easier than acquiring new ones, and if you have a proper retention strategy backed up by a CRM that can do the heavy lifting for you, your business is safe and sound.   (998 words)

(**Source:** https://www.reallysimplesystems.com/blog/crm-improves-customer-retention/.)

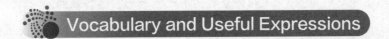

Vocabulary and Useful Expressions

re-engage /ˌriːɪnˈɡeɪdʒ/	v.	to become involved, or have contact, with someone or something again, for a second, third, etc. time 再接触，再参与
hibernation /ˌhaɪbɜːˈneɪʃən/	n.	cessation from or slowing of activity during the winter; especially slowing of metabolism in some animals 冬眠，休眠
exquisite /ɪkˈskwɪzɪt/	a.	extremely beautiful or pleasant, especially in a delicate way 精致的，精美的
shove /ʃʌv/	v.	to put sth. somewhere roughly or carelessly 乱放，随便放，胡乱丢，随手扔
perk /pɜːk/	n.	something you receive as well as your wages for doing a particular job （工资之外的）补贴，津贴，额外待遇
solidify /səˈlɪdɪfaɪ/	v.	to become or to make sth. become more definite and less likely to change （使）变得坚定，变得稳固，巩固
vigilantly /ˈvɪdʒɪləntlɪ/	ad.	done in a very careful way to notice any signs of danger or trouble 警觉地

churn /tʃɜːn/	n.	a regular, quantifiable process or rate of change that occurs in a business over a period of time as existing customers are lost and new customers are added 客户变动（流失）
mundane /mʌnˈdeɪn/	a.	not interesting or exciting 单调的，平凡的
palette /ˈpælət/	n.	You can refer to the range of colours that are used by a particular artist or group of artists as their palette. 一组颜色，色彩范围
be reckoned with		to consider or treat sb./sth. as a serious opponent, problem, etc. 重视，认真处理
fine-tune /ˌfaɪnˈtjuːn/	v.	to make very small and precise changes to something in order to make it as successful or effective as it possibly can be 调整，使有规则，对进行微调
seamless /ˈsiːmləs/	a.	with no spaces or pauses between one part and the next （两部分之间）无空隙的，不停顿的
tap into		to make use of a source of energy, knowledge, etc. that already exists 利用，开发，发掘（已有的资源、知识等）

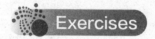

Exercises

Exercise 1. Language: Translate the following sentences into Chinese.

1. We need somebody to handle the marketing end of the business.

2. The management of the company are willing to make any concessions necessary to this end.

3. Tapping into social media to better your customer service is something you should seriously consider.

4. An e-mail marketing campaign powered by CRM data is a force to be reckoned with.

Unit 14 Customer Relationship Management

5. Connecting your marketing and sales teams is the key to creating a seamless customer experience.
   _____
   _____

6. One of the main problems of actual use of a CRM software can be its lack of integration with other tools.
   _____
   _____

7. As issues arise, you'll need to be able to handle all the tasks involved in their resolution.
   _____
   _____

8. An in-depth understanding of your customers' needs and wishes is the crucial element for a healthy relationship.
   _____
   _____

9. If you have a proper retention strategy backed up by a CRM that can do the heavy lifting for you, your business is safe and sound.
   _____
   _____

10. To form a healthy relationship with your customers, you need to be able to regard them as something more than just a source of profit.
    _____
    _____

Exercise 2. Knowledge: True or false statements. If the following statements are true, write T; if false, write F.

1. A CRM system is never located at the center of any good retention strategy. ( )
2. With service level agreements, the business and its customers can always be on the same page. ( )
3. A well implemented CRM can liberate marketers, enabling time to have more time to engage with customers. ( )
4. A major social media platform is a very valuable medium between the customer and businesses, therefore overlooking it will probably lower your customer service efficiency. ( )
5. Retaining customers is much more expensive and difficult than acquiring new ones, so new customer development is always the first priority of marketers. ( )
6. Integrating marketing and sales teams by a CRM will enable both teams to access to the

same information, which will definitely improve efficiency. ( )
7. SLAs will tell your customers what services you will provide, and how future situations will be handled, making them feel much safer. ( )
8. An e-mail marketing campaign powered by CRM data will make it highly targeted. ( )
9. An in-depth understanding of your customers' needs and wishes is the crucial element for a healthy relationship. ( )
10. Vigilantly tracking customer data will help avoid a high customer turnover rate and help retention of them. ( )

Exercise 3. Language: List some synonyms of the following words.
1. tap into: _____
2. fine tune: _____
3. vigilantly: _____
4. mundane: _____
5. solidify: _____
6. outcome: _____
7. monitor: _____
8. integration: _____
9. influential: _____
10. transparency: _____

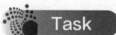

Oral practice: Work with your partners. Discuss the following questions and report your findings to the whole class.

1. What seems to be the major benefits of CRM? And what about the ultimate benefit of CRM?
2. Can CRM work alone to improve the business? Or shall it work with other parts of the business?
3. What are the major significance of CRM integrating with other major functions of business?

Text C: Extensive Reading

Successful vs. Failed CRM Implementation Cases[①]

Learning Resources

Adopting CRM can be very beneficial for the company's business in many aspects, but if wrongly implemented, it may also do harm to the well-being of one business. Let's firstly take a look at two successful cases and then a failed one. While you read, you may reflect and find out the secrets to CRM success or failure.

Two Successful Cases

1. Wells Fargo

Wells Fargo is a company tasked with keeping track of the property and assets of as many as 70 million people. To them, customer service has to be absolutely spot on. As one of the biggest banks in the US, Wells Fargo knows that in order to maintain their competitive edge, they need to go the extra mile when looking after clients.

In order to do this well, they make good use of CRM social media connectivity, enabling them to communicate easily with clients that need to talk to. Their CRM is also used to make certain that when problems arise, the issue is dealt with by the correct department within the organization. This eradicates the type of scenarios where clients are sent in circles, from department to department, endlessly trying to get an answer. The result is that they build fantastic relationships with clients, achieving a customer retention rate that is one of the best.

2. Activision

As a leading publisher in the US, Activision is heavily into the American video game market and has been so for more than three decades. Back in 2011, "Modern Warfare 3" achieved the title of being the "largest and most successful entertainment launch in history". Unbelievably, it made $400 million in just 24 hours! But Activision knew that money alone could not be their only measure of success.

They are very big on customer service, providing an unrivaled communication service to their gamers. The company's aim is to keep them happy even long after the purchase is made. By

---

① Adapted from an article by Jane Tareen.

using a CRM system, they monitor conversations within social media where they appertain to their products, following up to ensure that any problems are dealt with efficiently and positively. Because social media customer service is so affordable when compared with other methods, the company was able to reduce its customer service operating costs by 25%.

One Failed CRM Implementation Case

However, at times, some of the biggest businesses get it wrong when it comes to CRM.

This CRM case study took place a couple of years ago. A fairly large consulting firm needed some process design work to be carried out on their new CRM implementation. However, when they asked for help, the installation was already ongoing and the system was already being built.

The company made a decision to put in place the "best of breed" CRM system to automate its sales force. They also pulled in one of the world's largest CRM consulting firms to customize the software.

But things began to go wrong. The consulting firm quoted a figure of $20 million for them to design and customize the new CRM tool. The CIO (chief information officer) of the company felt that the price was much too high and threw it back at them. The result was devastating: the CRM consultants not only reduced the price but also lowered the scope of work, so that they would still make the same margin but do less work. The price was then reduced to $12 million, removing the process definition, business logic, and work flow, etc., all of which were the essential parts that the CRM was supposed to automate.

In fact, the CIO made a terrible mistake, believing that all these processes already existed or could be developed in-house. The fact was, they did not and the company had nothing to start with. Realizing their mistake, the company began to recruit hordes of additional consultants to take care of the creation and automation of the sales and marketing systems. Then the budget began to rapidly expand beyond the original figure of $20 million. Later the cost spiraled way out of control. In the end, the company spent $90 million on the CRM tool, paying the vendor $15 million and consultants $75 million!

But the worst thing is, no one in the company ever got to use the CRM as it was never successfully deployed. Years later as the economy slowed down, the company abandoned the system and finally went out of business.

Implications

These three cases reflected one fact: CRM can either be used incredibly well or exceptionally

Unit 14 Customer Relationship Management

badly.

This may be due to the fact that instead of seeing a CRM as an incredibly efficient piece of software that can dramatically increase a company's ROI, some companies see it as a magic cure. But in fact a CRM only enables systems to work better, it cannot resolve things that are going wrong. Before any type of CRM system is put in place, businesses of all sizes need to decide how they want the business processes to work before they're automated, and make sure that these processes actually exist.

A good idea is to begin with the basics and then add to what you have once it is working well. The most crucial part of using a CRM system is the work you do before it is deployed i.e. putting together a CRM selection team and then creating a detailed CRM requirements document, based upon precisely what your business needs. This should include the organization and automation of everything related to customer interaction, such as marketing, sales, customer service and customer support. The right CRM for your business will analyze all customer interactions and provide you with a way to improve and strengthen the customer relationship.   (962 words)

Writing: Read the above article and write down your answers to the following questions.

1. According to the first case, what is the major function of the CRM implemented by Wells Fargo? What type of CRM integration is adopted? What is its major objective? What is its major achievement?

   _____
   _____

2. According to the second case, what is the major function of the CRM implemented by Activision? What type of CRM integration is adopted?

   _____
   _____

3. According to the third case, what is the major cause of its failure of implementing the new CRM?

   _____
   _____

4. Write a summary of this article on the basis of your answers to the three questions.

   Word limit: 500 words.

Appendix A

Glossary

abuse /əˈbjuːs; əˈbjuːz/   n.   the use of sth. in a way that is wrong or harmful (~ of sth.) 滥用，妄用

abysmal /əˈbɪzməl/   a.   extremely bad or of a very low standard 极坏的，糟透的

academic /ˌækəˈdemɪk/   n.   scholar in university 学者

accessibility /əkˌsesəˈbɪlətɪ/   n.   the quality of being at hand when needed 易接近，可达性

address /əˈdres/   v.   (formal) to think about a problem or a situation and decide how you are going to deal with it (~ yourself to sth.) 设法解决，处理，对付

adolescence /ˌædəˈlesns/   n.   the time in a person's life when he or she develops from a child into an adult 青春期，青春

advocate /ˈædvəkeɪt/   n.   a person who supports or speaks in favour of sb. or of a public plan or action 拥护者，支持者，提倡者

aesthetic /iːsˈθetɪk/   n.   the aesthetic qualities and ideas of sth. 美感，审美观

algorithm /ˈælgərɪðəm/   n.   (especially computing) a set of rules that must be followed when solving a particular problem 算法，计算程序

225

allergic	/ə'lɜːdʒɪk/	a.	having an allergy to sth. (~ to sth.) （对……）过敏的
alternative	/ɔːl'tɜːnətɪv/	a.	(also alternate especially in North American English) that can be used instead of sth. else 可供替代的
ambush	/'æmbʊʃ/	n.	the act of hiding and waiting for sb. and then making a surprise attack on them 伏击，埋伏
analogy	/ə'nælədʒɪ/	n.	a comparison of one thing with another thing that has similar features; a feature that is similar (~ between A and B; ~ with sth.) 类比，比拟，比喻
ardent	/'ɑːdnt/	a.	very enthusiastic and showing strong feelings about sth./sb. 热烈的，激情的
association	/əˌsəʊsɪ'eɪʃn/	n.	an idea or a memory that is suggested by sb./sth.; a mental connection between ideas 联想，联系
at odds			to disagree with sb. about sth. (be ~ with sb.; be ~ over/on sth.) （就某事）（与某人）有分歧
attainable	/ə'teɪnəbl/	a.	that you can achieve 可达到的，可获得的
attribute	/ə'trɪbjuːt/	n.	a quality or feature of sb./sth. 属性，性质，特征
authenticity	/ˌɔːθen'tɪsətɪ/	n.	the quality of being genuine or true 真实性，确实性
aversion	/ə'vɜːʃn/	n.	a strong feeling of not liking sb./sth. (~ to sb./sth.) 厌恶，憎恶
be reckoned with			to consider or treat sb./sth. as a serious opponent, problem, etc. 重视，认真处理
blessing	/'blesɪŋ/	n.	something that is good or helpful 好事，有益之事
bloc	/blɒk/	n.	a group of countries that work closely together because they have similar political interests （政治利益一致的）国家集团
blueprint	/'bluːprɪnt/	n.	a plan which shows what can be achieved and how it can be achieved (~ for sth.) 行动方案，计划蓝图
branding	/'brændɪŋ/	n.	the activity of giving a particular name and image to goods and services so that people will be attracted to them and want to buy them 品牌建设，品牌推广
bribe	/braɪb/	n.	a sum of money or sth. valuable that you give or offer to sb. to persuade them to help you, especially

by doing sth. dishonest 贿赂

build /bɪld/   *n.* someone's build is the shape that their bones and muscles give to their body 体形，体格，身材

capitalize on   to gain a further advantage for yourself from a situation 充分利用，从……中获得更多的好处

capture /ˈkæptʃə(r)/   *v.* if you capture something that you are trying to obtain in competition with other people, you succeed in obtaining it 夺得，获得，得到

catalyst /ˈkætəlɪst/   *n.* a person or thing that causes a change (~ for sth.) 促使变化的人，引发变化的因素

cause /kɔːz/   *n.* an organization or idea that people support or fight for （支持或为之奋斗的）事业，目标，思想

cease /siːs/   *v.* (formal) to stop happening or existing; to stop sth. from happening or existing （使）停止，终止，结束

celebrity /səˈlebrəti/   *n.* someone who is famous, especially in areas of entertainment such as films, music, writing, or sport 名人，明星

chic /ʃiːk/   *a.* very fashionable and elegant 时髦的，优雅的，雅致的

churn /tʃɜːn/   *n.* a regular, quantifiable process or rate of change that occurs in a business over a period of time as existing customers are lost and new customers are added 客户变动（流失）

circumvent /ˌsɜːkəmˈvent/   *v.* to find a way of avoiding a difficulty or a rule 设法回避，规避

cliché /ˈkliːʃeɪ/   *n.* a phrase or an idea that has been used so often that it no longer has much meaning and is not interesting 陈词滥调，陈腐的套语

code /kəʊd/   *n.* a system of words, letters, numbers or symbols that represent a message or record information secretly or in a shorter form 密码，代码

   v. to write or print words, letters, numbers, etc. on sth. so that you know what it is, what group it belongs to, etc. 为……编码

cohesive /kəʊˈhiːsɪv/   *a.* forming a united whole 结成一个整体的

coin /kɔɪn/   *v.* to invent a new word or phrase that other people

			then begin to use 创造（新词语）
commercial	/kəˈmɜːʃl/	n.	an advertisement on the radio or on television （电台或电视播放的）广告
commercialization	/kəˌmɜːʃəlaɪˈzeɪʃn/	n.	the act of commercializing something; involving something in commerce 商品化
complement	/ˈkɒmplɪmənt/	v.	to add to sth. in a way that improves it or makes it more attractive 补充，补足，使完美，使更具吸引力
component	/kəmˈpəʊnənt/	n.	one of several parts of which sth. is made 组成部分，成分，部件
comprise	/kəmˈpraɪz/	v.	if you say that something comprises or is comprised of a number of things or people, you mean it has them as its parts or members 包括，由……组成
configuration	/kənˌfɪɡəˈreɪʃn/	n.	the way in which something, such as a computer system or software, is organized to operate 配置
consensus	/kənˈsensəs/	n.	an opinion that all members of a group agree with 一致的意见，共识
considerable	/kənˈsɪdərəbl/	a.	(formal) great in amount, size, importance, etc. 相当多（或大、重要等）的
consist	/kənˈsɪst/	v.	to be formed from the things or people mentioned (~ of) 由……组成（或构成）
consistent	/kənˈsɪstənt/	a.	always behaving in the same way, or having the same opinions, standards, etc. 一致的，始终如一的
contentious	/kənˈtenʃəs/	a.	likely to cause disagreement between people 可能引起争论的
contingent	/kənˈtɪndʒənt/	a.	(formal) depending on sth. that may or may not happen (~ on/upon sth.) 依情况而定的
convert	/kənˈvɜːt/	v.	to change to a new religion, belief, opinion, etc., or to make someone do this （使人）转变为/转化为
copyright	/ˈkɒpiraɪt/	n.	if a person or an organization holds the copyright on a piece of writing, music, etc., they are the only people who have the legal right to publish, broadcast, perform it, etc., and other people must ask their permission to use it or any part of it 版权，著作权
counterfeit	/ˈkaʊntəfɪt/	v.	to make an exact copy of sth. in order to trick people

			into thinking that it is the real thing 伪造，仿造，制假
craftsmanship	/ˈkrɑːftsmənʃɪp/	n.	craftsmanship is the quality that something has when it is beautiful and has been very carefully made 精工细作
credibility	/ˌkredəˈbɪləti/	n.	the quality that sb./sth. has that makes people believe or trust them 可信性，可靠性
crunch	/krʌntʃ/	v.	to do a lot of calculations using a calculator or computer （用计算器或计算机大量地）处理（数字）
curve	/kɜːv/	n.	a line or surface that bends gradually; a smooth bend 曲线
cutting-edge	/ˌkʌtɪŋˈedʒ/	a.	in accord with the most fashionable ideas or style 最前沿的，尖端的
cybersquatting	/ˈsaɪbəskwɒtɪŋ/	n.	the buying of an Internet domain name that might be wanted by another person, business, or organization with the intention of selling it to them and making a profit 抢注网络域名
cynical	/ˈsɪnɪkl/	a.	not caring that sth. might hurt other people, if there is some advantage for you 只顾自己不顾他人的，见利忘义的
damages	/ˈdæmɪdʒɪz/	n.	(pl) an amount of money that a court decides should be paid to sb. by the person, company, etc. that has caused them harm or injury （法院判定的）损害赔偿金
de facto	/ˌdeɪ ˈfæktəʊ/	a.	(from Latin, formal) existing as a fact although it may not be legally accepted as existing （常用于名词前）实际上存在的（不一定合法）
deceptive	/dɪˈseptɪv/	a.	likely to make you believe sth. that is not true 欺骗性的，误导的，骗人的
dedicate	/ˈdedɪkeɪt/	v.	to give a lot of your time and effort to a particular activity or purpose because you think it is important 把……奉献给
defective	/dɪˈfektɪv/	a.	having a fault or faults; not perfect or complete 有缺点的，有缺陷的，有毛病的
deficiency	/dɪˈfɪʃnsi/	n.	the state of not having, or not having enough of, sth. that is essential 缺乏，缺少，不足
deliberate	/dɪˈlɪbərət/	a.	done on purpose rather than by accident 故意的，

蓄意的，存心的

demographic	/ˌdeməˈgræfɪk/	a.	of or relating to a statistic characterizing human populations (or segments of human populations broken down by age, sex, income, etc.) 人口统计（学）的
demography	/dɪˈmɒgrəfɪ/	n.	the changing number of births, deaths, diseases, etc. in a community over a period of time; the scientific study of these changes 人口统计，人口统计学
density	/ˈdensətɪ/	n.	the quality of being dense; the degree to which sth. is dense 密集，稠密
deter	/dɪˈtɜː(r)/	v.	to make sb. decide not to do sth. or continue doing sth., especially by making them understand the difficulties and unpleasant results of their actions 制止，阻止，威慑，使不敢
devise	/dɪˈvaɪz/	v.	to invent sth. new or a new way of doing sth. 发明，设计，想出
dietary	/ˈdaɪətərɪ/	a.	related to anything that concerns a person's diet 饮食的，有关饮食的
differentiate	/ˌdɪfəˈrenʃɪeɪt/	v.	a quality or feature that differentiates one thing from another makes the two things different 使……差异化
dip	/dɪp/	v.	to go downwards or to a lower level; to make sth. do this （使）下降，下沉
dispense	/dɪˈspens/	v.	When a chemist dispenses medicine, he or she prepares it, and gives or sells it to the patient or customer. 配（药），配（方），发（药）
disposable	/dɪˈspəʊzəbl/	a.	made to be thrown away after use 用后即丢弃的，一次性的
distinct	/dɪˈstɪŋkt/	a.	clearly different or of a different kind 截然不同的，有区别的
dominance	/ˈdɒmɪnəns/	n.	the dominance of a particular person or thing is the fact that they are more powerful, successful, or important than other people or things 支配，控制
dub	/dʌb/	v.	to give sb./sth. a particular name, often in a humorous or critical way 把……戏称为，给……起绰号
duplicate	/ˈdjuːplɪkeɪt/	n.	one of two or more things that are the same in every detail 完全一样的东西，复制品，副本

eclipse	/ɪˈklɪps/	v.	to make sb./sth. seem dull or unimportant by comparison 使失色，使相形见绌，使丧失重要性
edge	/edʒ/	n.	a slight advantage over sb./sth. (~ on/over sb./sth.) （微弱的）优势
elaborate	/ɪˈlæbərət/	a.	very complicated and detailed; carefully prepared and organized 复杂的，详尽的，精心制作的
elasticity	/ˌiːlæˈstɪsəti/	n.	in economics, the elasticity of something, especially the demand for a product, is the degree to which it changes in response to changes in circumstances （尤指产品需求的）弹性，灵活性，伸缩性
emergence	/ɪˈmɜːdʒəns/	n.	the emergence of something is the process or event of its coming into existence 出现，兴起
emotional	/ɪˈməʊʃənl/	a.	connected with people's feelings (= with the emotions) 感情的，情感的，情绪的
encapsulate	/ɪnˈkæpsəleɪt/	v.	(formal) to express the most important parts of sth. in a few words, a small space or a single object 简述，概括，压缩
encompass	/ɪnˈkʌmpəs/	v.	(formal) to include a large number or range of things 包含，包括，涉及（大量事物）
engage	/ɪnˈɡeɪdʒ/	v.	If you engage in an activity, you do it or are actively involved with it. 参加，参与
engaging	/ɪnˈɡeɪdʒɪŋ/	a.	interesting or pleasant in a way that attracts your attention 有趣的，令人愉快的，迷人的
entitle	/ɪnˈtaɪtl/	v.	to give sb. the right to have or to do sth. (~ sb. to sth.) 使享有权利，使符合资格
entrant	/ˈentrənt/	n.	a person or an animal that enters a race or a competition; a person that enters an exam 参赛者（或动物），考生
equity	/ˈekwəti/	n.	the value of a company's shares; the value of a property after all charges and debts have been paid （公司的）股本，资产净值
equivalent	/ɪˈkwɪvələnt/	n.	a thing, amount, word, etc. that is equivalent to sth. else (~ of/to sth.) 相等的东西，等量，对应词
esteem	/ɪˈstiːm/	n.	(formal) great respect and admiration; a good opinion of sb. 尊重，敬重，好评

English for Marketing

European Single Market			The European Single Market, Internal Market or Common Market is a single market comprising the 27 member states of the European Union (EU) as well as—with certain exceptions—Iceland, Liechtenstein, and Norway through the Agreement on the European Economic Area, and Switzerland through bilateral treaties. The single market seeks to guarantee the free movement of goods, capital, services, and people, known collectively as the "four freedom". 欧洲单一市场
exacerbate	/ɪgˈzæsəbeɪt/	v.	(formal) to make sth. worse, especially a disease or problem 使恶化，使加剧，使加重
exemplify	/ɪgˈzemplɪfaɪ/	v.	to be a typical example of sth. 是……的典型（或典范、榜样）
exert	/ɪgˈzɜːt/	v.	to use power or influence to affect sb./sth. 运用，行使，施加
exhaustive	/ɪgˈzɔːstɪv/	a.	including everything possible; very thorough or complete 详尽的，彻底的，全面的
exhilarating	/ɪgˈzɪləreɪtɪŋ/	a.	very exciting and enjoyable 使人兴奋的，令人激动的
exhortation	/ˌegzɔːˈteɪʃn/	n.	the act of exhorting; an earnest attempt at persuasion 规劝，敦促，告诫
existent	/ɪgˈzɪstənt/	a.	existing; real 存在的，实有的
expedite	/ˈekspədaɪt/	v.	(formal) to make a process happen more quickly 加快，加速
expertise	/ˌekspɜːˈtiːz/	n.	expert knowledge or skill in a particular subject, activity or job 专门知识，专门技能，专长
expiry	/ɪkˈspaɪəri/	n.	an ending of the period of time when an official document can be used, or when an agreement is valid （文件、协议等的）满期，届期，到期
exploratory	/ɪkˈsplɒrətri/	a.	done with the intention of examining sth. in order to find out more about it 探索的，探究的
exquisite	/ɪkˈskwɪzɪt/	a.	extremely beautiful or pleasant, especially in a delicate way 精致的，精美的
extras	/ˈekstrəz/	n.	things which are not necessary in a situation, activity, or object, but which make it more comfortable, useful, or enjoyable 额外之物，附加物

Appendix A Glossary

facilitate	/fəˈsɪlɪteɪt/	v.	(formal) to make an action or a process possible or easier 促进，促使，使便利
feasibility	/ˌfiːzəˈbɪlɪtɪ/	n.	the possibility and likeliness to be achieved 可行性
feasible	/ˈfiːzəbl/	a.	that is possible and likely to be achieved 可行的，行得通的
fickle	/ˈfɪkl/	a.	(of a person) often changing their mind in an unreasonable way so that you cannot rely on them （人）反复无常的
file a lawsuit			to start a process by which a court of law makes a decision to end a disagreement between people or organizations 提起诉讼，打官司
fine-tune	/ˌfaɪnˈtjuːn/	v.	to make very small and precise changes to something in order to make it as successful or effective as it possibly can be 调整，使有规则，对进行微调
fiscal	/ˈfɪskl/	a.	connected with government or public money, especially taxes 财政的，国库的
flea market			an outdoor market that sells second-hand (= old or used) goods at low prices 跳蚤市场（廉价出售旧物的露天市场）
fleet	/fliːt/	n.	a fleet of vehicles is a group of them, especially when they all belong to a particular organization or business, or when they are all going somewhere together 车队
flourish	/ˈflʌrɪʃ/	v.	to develop quickly and be successful or common 繁荣，昌盛，兴旺
foremost	/ˈfɔːməʊst/	a.	the most important or famous; in a position at the front 最重要的，最著名的，最前的
forger	/ˈfɔːdʒə(r)/	n.	a person who makes illegal copies of money, documents, etc. in order to cheat people 伪造者，犯伪造罪的人
formulate	/ˈfɔːmjʊleɪt/	v.	to create or prepare sth. carefully, giving particular attention to the details 制订，规划，构想，准备
franchising	/ˈfræntʃaɪzɪŋ/	n.	a form of marketing and distribution in which the owner of a business system (the franchisor) grants to an individual or group of individuals (the franchisee) the right to run a business selling a

			product or providing a service using the franchisor's business system 特许经营
fraudster	/ˈfrɔːdstə(r)/	n.	a person who commits fraud 犯欺诈罪者，犯欺骗罪者
function	/ˈfʌŋkʃn/	v.	to work in the correct way 起作用，正常工作，运转
functionality	/ˌfʌŋkʃəˈnælətɪ/	n.	the range of functions that a computer or other electronic system can perform 功能，功能性
game plan			a plan for success in the future, especially in sport, politics or business （尤指体育运动、政治或商业方面的）行动计划，方案，对策
gear	/gɪə(r)/	n.	the gear involved in a particular activity is the equipment or special clothing that you use （某一特定活动的）设备，服装
generic	/dʒəˈnerɪk/	a.	not using the name of the company that made it 无厂家商标的，无商标的
genuine	/ˈdʒenjʊɪn/	a.	real; exactly what it appears to be; not artificial 真的，名副其实的
good	/gʊd/	n.	something that helps sb./sth. 用处，好处，益处
gravity	/ˈgrævətɪ/	n.	the force which causes things to drop to the ground 重力，万有引力
hail	/heɪl/	v.	to describe sb./sth. as being very good or special, especially in newspapers, etc. 赞扬（或称颂）……为……（尤用于报纸等）
hibernation	/ˌhaɪbɜːˈneɪʃən/	n.	cessation from or slowing of activity during the winter; especially slowing of metabolism in some animals 冬眠，休眠
hierarchy	/ˈhaɪərɑːkɪ/	n.	a system that ideas or beliefs can be arranged into 层次体系
high street			the main street of a town, where most shops/stores, banks, etc. are 大街（城镇的主要商业街道）
hobbyist	/ˈhɒbɪɪst/	n.	(formal) a person who is very interested in a particular hobby （业余）爱好者
holographic	/ˌhɒləˈgræfɪk/	a.	connected with holograms 全息图的
homogeneous	/ˌhɒməˈdʒiːnɪəs/	a.	consisting of things or people that are all the same or all of the same type 由相同（或同类型）事物（或人）组成的，同种类的，同质化的

Appendix A Glossary

hospitality	/ˌhɒspɪˈtælətɪ/	n.	food, drink or services that are provided by an organization for guests, customers, etc. （款待客人、顾客等的）食物，饮料，服务 the hospitality industry (= hotels, restaurants, etc.) 招待性行业（如旅馆、饭店等）
hypothesis	/haɪˈpɒθəsɪs/	n.	an idea or explanation of sth. that is based on a few known facts but that has not yet been proved to be true or correct （有少量事实依据但未被证实的）假说，假设
identifiable	/aɪˌdentɪˈfaɪəbl/	a.	that can be recognized 可识别的，可辨认的
impulse	/ˈɪmpʌls/	n.	a sudden strong wish or need to do sth., without stopping to think about the results (~ to do sth.) 冲动，心血来潮，一时的念头
incentive	/ɪnˈsentɪv/	n.	something that encourages you to do sth. (~ for/to sb./sth.; ~ to do sth.) 激励，刺激，鼓励
inducement	/ɪnˈdjuːsmənt/	n.	something that is given to sb. to persuade them to do sth. (~ to sb.; ~ to do sth.) 引诱，刺激，诱因
inflation	/ɪnˈfleɪʃn/	n.	a general rise in the prices of services and goods in a particular country, resulting in a fall in the value of money; the rate at which this happens 通货膨胀，通胀率
infrastructure	/ˈɪnfrəstrʌktʃə(r)/	n.	the basic systems and services that are necessary for a country or an organization to run smoothly, for example buildings, transport and water and power supplies （国家或机构的）基础设施，基础建设
infringe	/ɪnˈfrɪndʒ/	v.	to limit sb.'s legal rights (~ on/upon sth.) 侵犯，侵害（合法权益）
ingenuity	/ˌɪndʒɪˈnjuːətɪ/	n.	the ability to invent things or solve problems in clever new ways 独创力，聪明才智，心灵手巧
ingredient	/ɪnˈgriːdiənt/	n.	one of the things from which sth. is made, especially one of the foods that are used together to make a particular dish 成分，（尤指烹饪）原料
initiative	/ɪˈnɪʃətɪv/	n.	a new plan for dealing with a particular problem or for achieving a particular purpose 倡议，新方案
insight	/ˈɪnsaɪt/	n.	an accurate and deep understanding of a complex situation or problem （对复杂形势或问题的）洞察，深入见解

inspiring	/ɪnˈspaɪərɪŋ/	*a.*	exciting and encouraging you to do or feel sth. 鼓舞人心的，激励的，启发灵感的
instrument	/ˈɪnstrəmənt/	*n.*	(formal) something that is used by sb. in order to achieve sth.; a person or thing that makes sth. happen 促成某事的人（或事物），手段
intangible	/ɪnˈtændʒəbl/	*a.*	that does not exist as a physical thing but is still valuable to a company 无形的（指没有实体存在的资本性资产）
integrate	/ˈɪntɪgreɪt/	*v.*	to combine two or more things so that they work together; to combine with sth. else in this way （使）合并，成为一体
intellectual property			(law) an idea, a design, etc. that sb. has created and that the law prevents other people from copying （法律）知识财产
intercept	/ˌɪntəˈsept/	*v.*	to stop sb./sth. that is going from one place to another from arriving 拦截，拦阻，截住
interface	/ˈɪntəfeɪs/	*n.*	(computing) the way a computer program presents information to a user or receives information from a user, in particular the layout of the screen and the menus （人机）界面（尤指屏幕布局和菜单）
intermediary	/ˌɪntəˈmiːdiəri/	*n.*	(between A and B) a person or an organization that helps other people or organizations to make an agreement by being a means of communication between them 中间人，调解人
internal combustion engine			an internal combustion engine is an engine that creates its energy by burning fuel inside itself 内燃机
interoperate	/ˌɪntəˈɒpəreɪt/	*v.*	to operate together 交互操作
interpersonal	/ˌɪntəˈpɜːsənl/	*a.*	connected with relationships between people 人际关系的，人际的
judicial	/dʒuˈdɪʃl/	*a.*	connected with a court, a judge or legal judgement 法庭的，法官的，审判的，司法的
kindle	/ˈkɪndl/	*v.*	to start burning; to make a fire start burning 开始燃烧，点燃
knockoff	/ˈnɒkɔːf/	*n.*	a cheap copy of a well-known product （廉价）冒牌货，仿制品
know-how	/ˈnəʊ haʊ/	*n.*	knowledge of the methods or techniques of doing

Appendix A Glossary

			something, especially something technical or practical 专门知识，技能，实际经验
landscape	/'lændskeɪp/	n.	A landscape is all the features that are important in a particular situation. 形势，情形，情状
legality	/liːˈɡæləti/	n.	the fact of being legal （不可数名词）合法（性）the legal aspect of an action or a situation （可数名词，常用复数）（某行为或情况的）法律方面
legislation	/ˌledʒɪsˈleɪʃn/	n.	the process of making and passing laws 立法，制定法律
legitimate	/lɪˈdʒɪtɪmət/	a.	allowed and acceptable according to the law 合法的，法律认可的，法定的
leverage	/ˈlevərɪdʒ/	v.	to use for gain; to exploit; to use (something) to maximum advantage 利用，充分利用
lexicology	/ˌleksɪˈkɒlədʒɪ/	n.	the study of the form, meaning and behaviour of words 词汇学
liability	/ˌlaɪəˈbɪləti/	n.	the state of being legally responsible for sth. (~ for sth.; ~ to do sth.) （法律上对某事物的）责任，义务
lounge	/laʊndʒ/	n.	a room for waiting in at an airport, etc. （机场等的）等候室
lure	/lʊə(r)/	v.	(disapproving) to persuade or trick sb. to go somewhere or to do sth. by promising them a reward 劝诱，引诱，诱惑
manipulate	/məˈnɪpjuleɪt/	v.	(disapproving) to control or influence sb./sth., often in a dishonest way so that they do not realize it （暗中）控制，操纵，影响
manipulative	/məˈnɪpjulətɪv/	a.	if you describe someone as manipulative, you disapprove of them because they skillfully force or persuade people to act in the way that they want 善于操纵的，会控制的，会摆布人的
mass-produced	/ˌmæs prəˈdjuːst/	a.	if something is mass-produced, it is made in large quantities, usually by machine 大批量生产的
measurement	/ˈmeʒəmənt/	n.	The measurement of the quality, value, or effect of something is the activity of deciding how great it is. （质量、价值或影响的）衡量，评估，估量
minimalist	/ˈmɪnɪməlɪst/	n.	of, relating to, or done in the style of minimalism 极简主义的

multivariate /ˌmʌltɪˈveərɪət/   *a.*   involving two or more variable quantities 多变量的

mundane /mʌnˈdeɪn/   *a.*   not interesting or exciting 单调的，平凡的

name-brand /neɪm brænd/   *a.*   relating to or being a product that is made by a well-known company 名牌的

noteworthy /ˈnəʊtwɜːði/   *a.*   deserving to be noticed or to receive attention because it is unusual, important or interesting 值得注意的，显著的，重要的

obsolescence /ˌɒbsəˈlesns/   *n.*   (formal) the state of becoming old-fashioned and no longer useful (= becoming obsolete) 过时，陈旧，淘汰

obsolete /ˈɒbsəliːt/   *a.*   no longer used because sth. new has been invented 淘汰的，废弃的，过时的

odyssey /ˈɒdəsi/   *n.*   (literary) a long journey full of experiences 艰苦的跋涉，漫长而充满风险的历程

operational /ˌɒpəˈreɪʃənl/   *a.*   connected with the way in which a business, machine, system, etc. works 操作的，运转的，运营的，业务的

optimal /ˈɒptɪməl/   *a.*   most desirable possible under a restriction expressed or implied 最佳的，最优的，最理想的

outperform /ˌaʊtpəˈfɔːm/   *v.*   to achieve better results than sb./sth. （效益上）超过，胜过

outreach /ˈaʊtriːtʃ/   *n.*   the activity of an organization that provides a service or advice to people in the community, especially those who cannot or are unlikely to come to an office, a hospital, etc. for help 外展服务（在服务机构以外的场所提供的社区服务等）

overload /ˌəʊvəˈləʊd/   *n.*   too much of sth. 过多，过量，超负荷

overshadow /ˌəʊvəˈʃædəʊ/   *v.*   to make sb./sth. seem less important, or successful 使显得逊色，使黯然失色

palette /ˈpælət/   *n.*   You can refer to the range of colours that are used by a particular artist or group of artists as their palette. 一组颜色，色彩范围

panel /ˈpænl/   *n.*   A panel is a small group of people who are chosen to do something, for example to discuss something in public or to make a decision. 专门小组

parallel /ˈpærəlel/   *a.*   very similar or taking place at the same time 极相似的，同时发生的

Appendix A Glossary

patent /ˈpeɪtnt; ˈpætnt/   *n.*   an official right to be the only person to make, use or sell a product or an invention; a document that proves this 专利权，专利证书

pension /ˈpenʃn/   *n.*   an amount of money paid regularly by a government or company to sb. who is considered to be too old or too ill/sick to work 养老金，退休金，抚恤金

perception /pəˈsepʃn/   *n.*   (formal) an idea, a belief or an image you have as a result of how you see or understand sth. 看法，见解

perk /pɜːk/   *n.*   something you receive as well as your wages for doing a particular job （工资之外的）补贴，津贴，额外待遇

persona /pəˈsəʊnə/   *n.*   the aspect of their character or nature that they present to other people 表象人格

perspective /pəˈspektɪv/   *n.*   a particular attitude towards sth.; a way of thinking about sth. (~ on sth.) 态度，观点，思考方法

pertain /pəˈteɪn/   *v.*   (formal) to be connected with sth./sb. 与……相关，关于

pharmaceutical /ˌfɑːməˈsuːtɪkl/   *a.*   connected with making and selling drugs and medicines 制药的，配药的，卖药的

pharmacy /ˈfɑːməsɪ/   *n.*   a shop/store, or part of one, that sells medicines and drugs 药房，药店，医药柜台

philanthropy /fɪˈlænθrəpɪ/   *n.*   the practice of helping the poor and those in need, especially by giving money 博爱，慈善，乐善好施

physiological /ˌfɪziəˈlɒdʒɪk(ə)l/   *a.*   of or relating to the biological study of physiology 生理学的，生理的

piracy /ˈpaɪrəsɪ/   *n.*   the act of making illegal copies of video tapes, computer programs, books, etc., in order to sell them 盗版行为，非法复制

pivotal /ˈpɪvətl/   *a.*   of great importance because other things depend on it 关键性的，核心的

poised /pɔɪzd/   *a.*   completely ready for sth. or to do sth. 有充分准备，准备好，蓄势待发

policy /ˈpɒləsɪ/   *n.*   a written statement of a contract of insurance 保险单

portray /pɔːˈtreɪ/   *v.*   to show sb./sth. in a picture; to describe sb./sth. in a piece of writing 描绘，描画，描写

positivity	/ˌpɒzɪˈtɪvɪtɪ/	n.	the practice of being or tendency to be positive or optimistic in attitude 积极性
practitioner	/prækˈtɪʃənə(r)/	n.	(formal) a person who regularly does a particular activity, especially one that requires skill 专门人才
pragmatic	/præɡˈmætɪk/	a.	solving problems in a practical and sensible way rather than by having fixed ideas or theories 实用的，讲求实效的，务实的
precedence	/ˈpresɪdəns/	n.	the condition of being more important than sb. else and therefore coming or being dealt with first 优先，优先权
prescription	/prɪˈskrɪpʃn/	n.	medicine that your doctor has ordered for you 医生开的药
prioritize	/praɪˈɒrətaɪz/	v.	to put tasks, problems, etc. in order of importance, so that you can deal with the most important first 按重要性排列，划分优先顺序
privilege	/ˈprɪvəlɪdʒ/	n.	a special right or advantage that a particular person or group of people has 特殊利益，优惠待遇
proactively	/ˌprəʊˈæktɪvlɪ/	ad.	controlling a situation in a way that makes things happen rather than waiting for things to happen and then reacting to them 积极主动地，主动出击地，先发制人地
proceed	/prəˈsiːd/	v.	to continue doing sth. that has already been started; to continue being done (~ with sth.) 继续做（或从事、进行）
procurement	/prəˈkjuəmənt/	n.	the process of obtaining supplies of sth., especially for a government or an organization （尤指为政府或机构）采购，购买
productivity	/ˌprɒdʌkˈtɪvətɪ/	n.	the rate at which a worker, a company or a country produces goods, and the amount produced, compared with how much time, work and money is needed to produce them 生产率，生产效率，生产力
professional	/prəˈfeʃənl/	n.	a person who does a job that needs special training and a high level of education 专门人员，专业人士，专家
profile	/ˈprəʊfaɪl/	n.	a description of sb./sth. that gives useful information 概述，简介，传略

Appendix A Glossary

prominent	/ˈprɒmɪnənt/	a.	something that is prominent is very noticeable or is an important part of something else 显著的，突出的，引人注目的
prospective	/prəˈspektɪv/	a.	expected to do sth. or to become sth. 有望的，可能成为的，预期的，潜在的
prototype	/ˈprəʊtətaɪp/	n.	the first design of sth. from which other forms are copied or developed (~ for/of sth.) 原型，雏形，最初形态
psychographic	/ˌsaɪkəʊˈɡræfɪk/	a.	concerning the study of customers in relation to their opinions, interests, and emotions （有关）消费者心理特征的
publics	/ˈpʌblɪks/	n.	Publics are small groups of people who follow one or more particular issue very closely. 公众，……界
quest	/kwest/	n.	(formal, or literary) a long search for sth., especially for some quality such as happiness (~ for sth.) 探索，寻找，追求（幸福等）
questionnaire	/ˌkwestʃəˈneə(r)/	n.	a written list of questions that are answered by a number of people so that information can be collected from the answers (~ on/about sth.) 调查表，问卷
rational	/ˈræʃnəl/	a.	(of behaviour, ideas, etc.) based on reason rather than emotions （行为、思想等）合理的，理性的，明智的
recency	/ˈriːsnsɪ/	n.	the property of having happened or appeared not long ago（as in primacy-recency effect, 首因－近因效应）近因
recession	/rɪˈseʃn/	n.	a difficult time for the economy of a country, when there is less trade and industrial activity than usual and more people are unemployed 经济衰退，经济萎缩
reciprocity	/ˌresɪˈprɒsətɪ/	n.	(formal) a situation in which two people, countries, etc. provide the same help or advantages to each other 互惠，互助，互换
recognizable	/ˌrekəɡˈnaɪzəbl/	a.	easy to know or identify 容易认出的，易于识别的
re-engage	/ˌriːɪnˈɡeɪdʒ/	v.	to become involved, or have contact, with someone or something again, for a second, third, etc. time

			再接触，再参与
renew	/rɪˈnjuː/	v.	to make sth. valid for a further period of time 使继续有效，延长……的期限
renewable	/rɪˈnjuːəbl/	a.	that is replaced naturally or controlled carefully and can therefore be used without the risk of finishing it all 可更新的，可再生的，可恢复的
replacement	/rɪˈpleɪsmənt/	n.	a thing that replaces sth., especially because the first thing is old, broken, etc. 替代品，替换物
resonate	/ˈrezəneɪt/	v.	to remind sb. of sth.; to be similar to what sb. thinks or believes (~ with sb./sth.) 使产生联想，引起共鸣
respondent	/rɪˈspɒndənt/	n.	a person who answers questions, especially in a survey 回答问题的人，（尤指）调查对象
revamp	/ˌriːˈvæmp/	v.	make changes to something in order to try and improve it 修补，修改，改进
revenue	/ˈrevənjuː/	n.	money that a company, organization, or government receives from people （公司、组织的）收入，收益，（政府的）财政收入，税收
ROI			return on investment 投资回报
roll-out	/ˈrəʊlˌaʊt/	n.	an occasion when a company introduces or starts to use a new product 新产品发布会，新产品的推出
route	/ruːt/	n.	a particular way of achieving sth. (~ to sth.) 途径，渠道
saturated	/ˈsætʃəreɪtɪd/	a.	if the market for a product is saturated, there is more of the product available than there are people who want to buy it （市场）饱和的
savvy	/ˈsævɪ/	n.	(informal) practical knowledge or understanding of sth. 实际知识，见识，了解
scale	/skeɪl/	n.	a range of levels or numbers used for measuring sth. 等级，级别
scheme	/skiːm/	n.	(British English) a plan or system for doing or organizing sth. 计划，方案，体系，体制
screen	/skriːn/	v.	to check sth. to see if it is suitable or if you want it 审查，筛选
scrutinize	/ˈskruːtənaɪz/	v.	to look at or examine sb./sth. carefully 仔细查看，认真检查，细致审查

seamless	/ˈsiːmləs/	*a.*	with no spaces or pauses between one part and the next （两部分之间）无空隙的，不停顿的
segmentation	/ˌsegmenˈteɪʃn/	*n.*	(technical) the act of dividing sth. into different parts; one of these parts （术语）分割，细分
self-actualization	/ˌself ˌæktʃʊəlaɪˈzeɪʃən/	*n.*	the process of establishing oneself as a whole person, able to develop one's abilities and to understand oneself 自我实现
session	/ˈseʃn/	*n.*	A session of a particular activity is a period of that activity. （某项活动的）一段时间，一场，一节
shelter	/ˈʃeltə(r)/	*n.*	the fact of having a place to live or stay, considered as a basic human need 居所，住处
shorthand	/ˈʃɔːthænd/	*n.*	a shorter way of saying or referring to sth., which may not be as accurate as the more complicated way of saying it (~ for sth.) （对某事）简略的表达方式
shove	/ʃʌv/	*v.*	to put sth. somewhere roughly or carelessly 乱放，随便放，胡乱丢，随手扔
shrink	/ʃrɪŋk/	*v.*	to become or to make sth. smaller in size or amount （使）缩小，收缩，减少
shrivel	/ˈʃrɪvl/	*v.*	to become or make sth. dry and wrinkled as a result of heat, cold or being old [~ sth. (up)] （使）枯萎，干枯，皱缩
silo	/ˈsaɪləʊ/	*n.*	a tall tower on a farm used for storing grain, etc. 筒仓
simulation	/ˌsɪmjuˈleɪʃn/	*n.*	a situation in which a particular set of conditions is created artificially in order to study or experience sth. that could exist in reality 模拟，仿真
simultaneously	/ˌsɪməlˈteɪnɪəslɪ/	*ad.*	at the same time 同时地
skilled	/skɪld/	*a.*	having enough ability, experience and knowledge to be able to do sth. well 有技能的，熟练的
sociocultural	/ˌsəʊsɪəʊˈkʌltʃərəl/	*a.*	relating to both social and cultural matters 社会文化的
solidify	/səˈlɪdɪfaɪ/	*v.*	to become or to make sth. become more definite and less likely to change （使）变得坚定，变得稳固，巩固
specification	/ˌspesɪfɪˈkeɪʃn/	*n.*	a detailed description of how sth. is, or should be, designed or made 规格，规范，明细单，说明书

spectrum	/ˈspektrəm/	n.	a complete or wide range of related qualities, ideas, etc. 范围，各层次
stabilize	/ˈsteɪbəlaɪz/	v.	to become or to make sth. become firm, steady and unlikely to change; to make sth. stable （使）稳定，稳固
stakeholder	/ˈsteɪkhəʊldə(r)/	n.	a person or company that is involved in a particular organization, project, system, etc., especially because they have invested money in it （某组织、工程、体系等的）参与人，参与方，有权益关系者，利益相关者
startup	/ˈstɑːtʌp/	n.	a company that has been newly established for business 初创公司
statistics	/stəˈtɪstɪks/	n.	a collection of information shown in numbers 统计数字，统计资料
stiff	/stɪf/	a.	more difficult or severe than usual 困难的，艰难的，严厉的，激烈的
stratosphere	/ˈstrætəsfɪə(r)/	n.	If you say that someone or something climbs or is sent into the stratosphere, you mean that they reach a very high level. 最高层，最高水平，顶峰（原意：平流层）
stray	/streɪ/	v.	if your mind or your eyes stray, you do not concentrate on or look at one particular subject, but start thinking about or looking at other things 走神，（视线）偏离，往别处看
subscriber	/səbˈskraɪbə(r)/	n.	a person who pays to receive a service 消费者，用户
subsidize	/ˈsʌbsɪdaɪz/	v.	to give money to sb. or an organization to help pay for sth.; to give a subsidy 资助，补助，给……发津贴
subsidy	/ˈsʌbsədi/	n.	money that is paid by a government or an organization to reduce the costs of services or of producing goods so that their prices can be kept low 补贴，补助金，津贴
subsistence	/səbˈsɪstəns/	n.	the state of having just enough money or food to stay alive 勉强维持生活
suppress	/səˈpres/	v.	to prevent yourself from having or expressing a feeling or an emotion 抑制，控制，忍住

Appendix A Glossary

surpass	/sə'pɑːs/	v.	(formal) to do or be better than sb./sth. 超过，胜过，优于
surveillance	/sɜː'veɪləns/	n.	the act of carefully watching a person suspected of a crime or a place where a crime may be committed （对犯罪嫌疑人或可能发生犯罪的地方的）监视
sustain	/sə'steɪn/	v.	to make sth. continue for some time without becoming less; to provide enough of what sb./sth. needs in order to live or exist 使保持，使稳定持续，维持（生命、生存）
sustainable	/sə'steɪnəbl/	a.	involving the use of natural products and energy in a way that does not harm the environment 不破坏生态平衡的，合理利用的
sustained	/səs'teɪnd/	a.	maintained at length without interruption or weakening 可持续的，持久的
switch	/swɪtʃ/	v.	to change or make sth. change from one thing to another (~ sth. over/ from sth. to sth.; ~ between A and B) （使）改变，转变，突变
synonymous	/sɪ'nɒnɪməs/	a.	having the same, or nearly the same, meaning 同义的
systematic	/ˌsɪstə'mætɪk/	a.	done according to a system or plan, in a thorough, efficient or determined way 成体系的，系统的，有条理的，有计划、有步骤的
tangible	/'tændʒəbl/	a.	that can be clearly seen to exist 有形的，实际的，真实的
tap into			to make use of a source of energy, knowledge, etc. that already exists 利用，开发，发掘（已有的资源、知识等）
tense	/tens/	a.	nervous or worried, and unable to relax 神经紧张的，担心的，不能松弛的
territory	/'terətrɪ/	n.	land that is under the control of a particular country or ruler 领土，版图，领地
toolkit	/'tuːlkɪt/	n.	a set of tools in a box or bag （装在箱子或包里的）一套工具，工具箱，工具包
trademark	/'treɪdmɑːk/	n.	a name, symbol or design that a company uses for its products and that cannot be used by anyone else 商标
trainee	/ˌtreɪ'niː/	n.	a person who is being taught how to do a particular

job 接受培训者，实习生

transactional /trænˈzækʃənəl/   *a.* relating to the conducting of business, especially buying or selling 交易的

ubiquitous /juːˈbɪkwɪtəs/   *a.* seeming to be everywhere or in several places at the same time; very common 似乎无所不在的，十分普遍的

undergo /ˌʌndəˈɡəʊ/   *v.* to experience sth., especially a change or sth. unpleasant 经历，经受（变化、不快的事等）

undertake /ˌʌndəˈteɪk/   *v.* to make yourself responsible for sth. and start doing it 承担，从事，负责

undifferentiated /ˌʌnˌdɪfəˈrenʃɪeɪtɪd/   *a.* having parts that you cannot distinguish between; not split into different parts or sections 无法区分的，分不开的，一体的

univariate /ˌjuːnɪˈveərɪət/   *a.* involving one variate or variable quantity 单变量的

unmet /ˌʌnˈmet/   *a.* (formal) (of needs, etc.) not satisfied （需要等）未满足的

unproven /ˌʌnˈpruːvn/   *a.* not proved or tested 未验证的，未经检验的

unwind /ˌʌnˈwaɪnd/   *v.* to stop worrying or thinking about problems and start to relax 放松，轻松

upscale /ˌʌpˈskeɪl/   *a.* Upscale is used to describe products or services that are expensive, of good quality, and intended to appeal to people in a high social class. （产品或服务）高档的，质优价高的

user interface   (computer science) a program that controls a display for the user (usually on a computer monitor) and that allows the user to interact with the system （计算机）用户界面

variable /ˈveərɪəbl/   *n.* a situation, number or quantity that can vary or be varied 可变情况，变量，可变因素

verification /ˌverɪfɪˈkeɪʃn/   *n.* the process of establishing the truth, accuracy, or validity of something 验证

viability /ˌvaɪəˈbɪlətɪ/   *n.* the ability to continue to exist or develop (as a product, for example) 生存能力

vigilantly /ˈvɪdʒɪləntlɪ/   *ad.* done in a very careful way to notice any signs of danger or trouble 警觉地